jazz
theory

jazz
theory

andrew jaffe

wcb

WM. C. BROWN COMPANY PUBLISHERS
Dubuque, Iowa

Consulting Editor
Frederick W. Westphal
California State University, Sacramento

Cover photo courtesy of CBS

Copyright © 1983 by Wm. C. Brown Company Publishers

Library of Congress Catalogue Card Number: 82-72110

ISBN 0-697-03549-2

Printed in the United States of America

2-03549-01

contents

preface

In 1976, while teaching a course in jazz theory and improvisation at the University of Massachusetts, I became aware of the need for a comprehensive text on the subject. Like many instructors in this area at the college level, I found myself resorting to a combination of materials: those which I was forced to develop myself and many different secondary materials in the form of books of exercises, scales, and so on. I found the many publications by such authors as Coker, Baker, and Tirro excellent in their approach to the specific theoretical or historical topics they addressed, but not comprehensive concerning the entire spectrum of topics for a full program of classroom jazz instruction. A stint at Boston's Berklee College of Music teaching theory further convinced me of the need for such a text. I received many queries from my students there concerning a good basic theory text they could use as a reference to supplement their course notes. It therefore seemed to me that the need for such a text existed on the part of both students and faculty alike, and Wm. C. Brown Company Publishers agreed. The current text is a result of a great deal of hard work on their part, as well as my own.

The text considers three areas in the study of jazz: by (1) theory, (2) practice, and (3) reference materials. Each chapter begins with a theoretical discussion of the given topic, followed by exercises designed to provide not only practical application of the knowledge just acquired, but also models for other similar supplementary exercises. At the close of each chapter, a discography lists recordings of each composition cited in the chapter, which I have selected to provide as wide a variety as possible of representative jazz styles. Also at the close of each chapter a bibliography lists relevant supplementary materials such as exercises and methods books, shorter theory books, and lesser known source materials such as magazine articles, doctoral theses, and books of transcriptions.

An instructor's manual accompanies the text; it explains the common pitfalls in teaching each topic, based on my experience over the past few years. The instructor's manual also suggests timing and content for exams and student projects, as well as ideas for supplemental projects and lecture examples. It is my hope that the instructor will be able to set up an entire library of tapes and resource materials for a jazz theory course on the basis of the excellent bibliography in the text, and that the instructor's manual will make it clear exactly how to employ these materials in teaching the course. From the students' point of view, this text offers an opportunity to have not just the facts of the music presented, but their theoretical basis and explanation as well.

Before closing this preface, I would be remiss were I not to thank the many individuals without whom this text would not exist: Catherine Collins, music librarian at the University of Massachusetts, whose thorough and knowledgeable work resulted in the bibliography and discography for this text; Wade Clark, of Minneapolis, Minnesota, whose steady hand and patient eye deciphered my various illustrations and brought them to you in their currently legible form; Drucilla Wood, whose editorial and typing skills did the same for my insufferably convoluted paragraphs; the editors with whom I've worked at Wm. C. Brown, without whom none of this would exist in its present form—Louise Waller and Kevin Kane; the many jazz educators with whom it has been my pleasure to associate—Dr. Frederick Tillis and Max Roach of the University of Massachusetts, Amherst; Dr. John Maggs of Amherst, Massachusetts; the many fine educators and musicians on the faculty at Boston's Berklee College of Music; and, finally, Wm. C. Brown's fine team of consulting editors lead by Dr. Fred Westphal.

It is my strong conviction that it is time for jazz, America's truly *classical* music, to be given the recognition in our own academic and artistic institutions that it has been given throughout the rest of the world. Music educators can accomplish a great deal by working together, and it is my hope that this text, and the many excellent works cited in its bibliography and discography, can function as an effective unit in helping us all to bring a greater level of understanding to America's greatest music.

intervals and scale
and chord construction

1

This chapter reviews the basic principles of interval identification and nomenclature and discusses the mechanics by which intervals are combined to form scales and chords. The descriptions for these basic building blocks of musical construction as used in the theory and practice of jazz may differ from those you have learned in traditional music theory. Therefore, it is important that the primary definitions of our new theoretical language are entirely clear.

First, all scales and chords are built with *intervals*. An interval is defined as the distance, in pitch, between any two notes. These distances are expressed in terms of the *half step,* the smallest interval in common use in Western instrumental music and therefore the common denominator among intervals. The term *chromatic* is often used to describe two adjacent pitches. The following illustration of a portion of the piano keyboard in example 1.1 shows all of the discrete half step intervals as well as the different descriptions for each pitch involved.

Example 1.1.

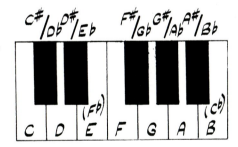

The above illustration is described in musical notation as it appears in examples 1.2 and 1.3.

Example 1.2.

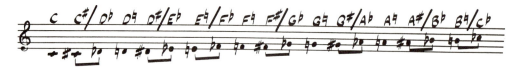

Or,

Example 1.3.

These three examples illustrate the most basic type of scale. This is the *chromatic scale* and is produced by playing all of the twelve adjacent pitches in ascending or descending order.

As you can see, more than one description may exist for any pitch. This phenomenon, known as *enharmonics,* refers to the existence of two or more designations for the same pitch. These designations are said to be enharmonic as, for example, C♯ is an enharmonic spelling for D♭. These descriptions are frequently interchanged, particularly when chords and key centers change. Because this occurs so often in jazz, it is important to have a thorough mastery of enharmonic spelling.

Using middle C as an arbitrary point of reference, we see twelve intervals possible between it and the remaining notes in the chromatic scale. Each interval contains an increasing number of half steps as we move further from middle C. Consulting the keyboard illustration from example 1.1, play each of these intervals and try to learn their sounds. The ability to identify these intervals when they occur melodically or harmonically is one of the most important skills you can develop in attempting to master a musical art form that is based primarily in aural tradition. Many people use fragments of common melodies as crutches for purposes of intervallic comparison. For example, "My Bonnie Lies Over the Ocean" begins with a major sixth, and Leonard Bernstein's "Maria" begins with an augmented fourth. Table 1.1 indicates all such intervals and their descriptions.

Note that when two names are possible for a given interval, it is theoretically more correct to use the description implied by the enharmonic spelling of the upper note of the pair. For example, it is more correct to call the interval C to D♯ an augmented second than a minor third, since C to D is technically some sort of a second, regardless of which *kind* of a D it is. Similarly, C to E♭ must be a minor third. In actual jazz practice, however, such strictures are not always observed, and students should be able to translate freely between academically correct and enharmonic usages.

Table 1.1.

Pitch of Origin	Destination	Interval Name(s)	Number of Half Steps
Middle C	Db/C♯	Half step; minor second	1
Middle C	D	Whole step; major second	2
Middle C	D♯/Eb	Augmented second; minor third	3
Middle C	E	Major third	4
Middle C	F	Perfect fourth	5
Middle C	F♯/Gb	Augmented fourth; diminished fifth; "tritone"	6
Middle C	G	Perfect fifth	7
Middle C	G♯/Ab	Augmented fifth; minor sixth	8
Middle C	A	Major sixth	9
Middle C	A♯/Bb	Augmented sixth*; minor seventh	10
Middle C	B	Major seventh	11
Middle C	C'	One octave	12

*This intervallic description is not in common use in jazz and popular harmony.

The intervals listed in table 1.1 are *simple* intervals, that is, they are smaller than one *octave*. An octave is the distance between any pitch and that same pitch as it next occurs as one moves up or down from it—or twelve half steps. Intervals larger than the octave are known as *compound* intervals, and their nomenclature is obtained by adding seven to the simple interval description. For example, the distance from any C to the D an octave and one whole step higher would be a major second (C to D) plus seven, or a major ninth. Note that the quality of the interval, for example, major, minor, or perfect, is retained in the compound interval nomenclature. Table 1.2 indicates the various compound interval descriptions most commonly used. Compound interval nomenclature becomes extremely important in discussions of the more sophisticated harmonic phenomena associated with chord voicings indigenous to the jazz idiom.

When we hear an interval, we may have difficulty in telling which of its two pitches is the point of origin. We might hear the pitches A and C♯, for example, and be unsure as to whether the interval created is a major third or a minor sixth. The obvious and strong relationship between these two intervals is known as *inversion*. Table 1.3 summarizes these relationships for the simple and compound intervals discussed up to this point.

It must be emphasized that these intervallic relationships do not apply solely to the tonal center of C. They are generic, applying regardless of the particular pitch used as point of origin. Also note the commonly used abbreviations for the various

Table 1.2.

Pitch of Origin	Destination (plus 1 octave)		Compound Interval	Number of Half Steps
C	C♯/D♭	m2nd(+7)	♭9	13
C	D	M2nd(+7)	9	14
C	D♯/E♭	m3rd(+7)	♯9	15
C	E	M3rd(+7)	10th	16
C	F	P4th(+7)	11th	17
C	F♯/G♭	+4th(+7)	♯11th	18
C	G	P5th(+7)	12th	19
C	G♯/A♭	m6th(7+)	♭13th	20
C	A	M6th(+7)	13th	21
C	A♯/B♭	m7th(+7)	*	22
C	B	M7th(+7)	*	23

*No commonly used description exists.

Table 1.3.

Pitch of Origin	Destination	Interval Name(s)	Interval's Inversion
Middle C	D♭/D	m2	Inverts to M7
Middle C	D	M2	Inverts to m7
Middle C	D♯/E♭	+2/m3	Inverts to M6
Middle C	E	M3	Inverts to m6
Middle C	F	P4	Inverts to P5
Middle C	F♯/G♭	+4/dim 5 (tritone)	= dim 5/+4 (tritone)
Middle C	G	P5	Inverts to P4
Middle C	G♯/A♭	+5/m6	Inverts to M3
Middle C	A	M6	Inverts to m3
Middle C	A♯/B♭	+6/m7	Inverts to M2
Middle C	B	M7	Inverts to m2
Middle C	C'	Octave (8ve)	Inverts to unison

intervals. While *major* intervals invert to *minor,* and *augmented* intervals to *diminished, perfect* intervals remain unchanged in quality when inverted. Obviously, this entire process becomes more involved with the introduction of three- and four-note structures and their various intervallic permutations.

We may derive interval formulas to construct and define all commonly used vertical (chordal) and horizontal (scalar) structures, although we may also think of chords as being generated by scales. By far the most common scale in use in Western instrumental music is the *major scale,* also known as the *ionian mode.* Its interval formula is expressed in steps and half steps as seen in Example 1.4.

Example 1.4.

Shifting this same scale to start on each of its individual degrees produces a displacement of the sequence of original step and half-step relationships, without changing any of the individual pitches involved. These six transpositions of the root of the scale to its varying degrees are known collectively as the *diatonic modes.* Diatonic, originally a Greek word, simply means "belonging to the scale." The family of diatonic modes shown in table 1.4 derives from the C major scale. You should become familiar with the characteristic sound of each mode, which will be determined by its unique intervallic succession of steps and half steps. You should also learn the names of the seven different modes that are associated with each of the twelve different families in the major keys. Table 1.4 lists the family of diatonic modes in the key of C. Each mode is accompanied by an interval formula, and individual pitches within each mode are labelled.

Table 1.4.

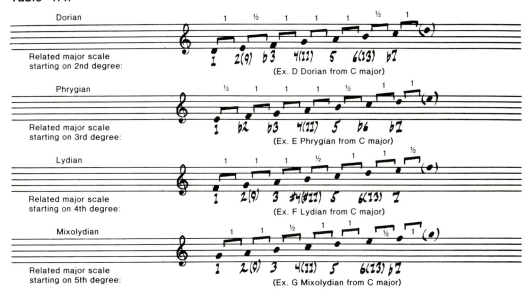

Table 1.4—*Continued*

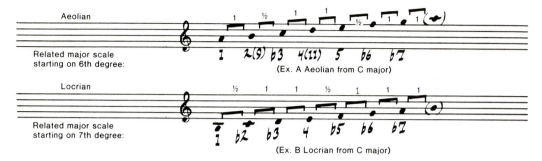

Aeolian

Related major scale starting on 6th degree:

1   2(9) ♭3 4(11) 5   ♭6   ♭7

(Ex. A Aeolian from C major)

Locrian

Related major scale starting on 7th degree:

1   ♭2 ♭3 4   ♭5 ♭6 ♭7

(Ex. B Locrian from C major)

Note that a mode is named after the pitch it actually starts *on* and not the scale *from* which it was diatonically derived.

In addition to the basic diatonic modes, you should also become familiar with the commonly used scales in table 1.5.

Table   1.5.

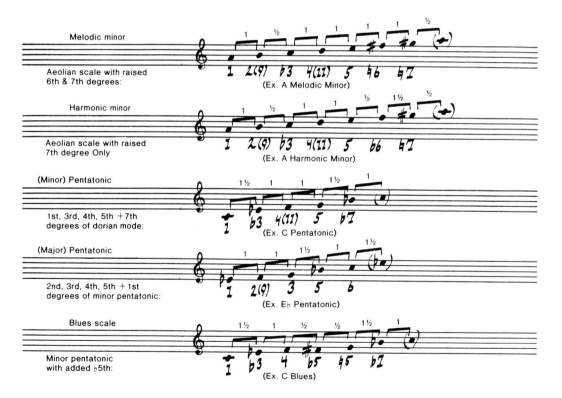

Melodic minor

Aeolian scale with raised 6th & 7th degrees:

1   2(9) ♭3 4(11) 5   ♮6   ♮7

(Ex. A Melodic Minor)

Harmonic minor

Aeolian scale with raised 7th degree Only

1   2(9) ♭3 4(11) 5   ♭6   ♮7

(Ex. A Harmonic Minor)

(Minor) Pentatonic

1st, 3rd, 4th, 5th +7th degrees of dorian mode:

1   ♭3 4(11) 5   ♭7

(Ex. C Pentatonic)

(Major) Pentatonic

2nd, 3rd, 4th, 5th +1st degrees of minor pentatonic:

1   2(9) 3   5   6

(Ex. E♭ Pentatonic)

Blues scale

Minor pentatonic with added ♭5th:

1   ♭3 4   ♭5 ♮5 ♭7

(Ex. C Blues)

Table 1.5—*Continued*

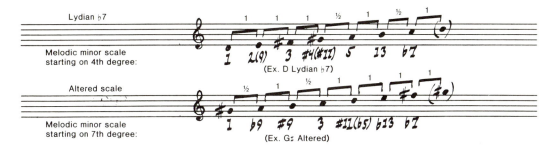

Lydian ♭7

Melodic minor scale starting on 4th degree:

(Ex. D Lydian ♭7)

Altered scale

Melodic minor scale starting on 7th degree:

(Ex. G♯ Altered)

Musical competency requires fluency in transposing this theoretical information and applying it in any key. Of equal importance to our knowledge of basic scales and intervals is an understanding of the basic chord types associated with them. While a *scale* is the horizontal expression of various interval combinations, *chords* constitute particular vertical combinations of intervals. In Western instrumental music, chords commonly have been built from various combinations of major and minor thirds. Since the interval formula for the major scale and its related family of modes features an alternation of steps and half steps, the type of third, and hence the resultant chord type that can be derived diatonically, will depend upon where within the scale this process takes place. Building chords in thirds (to do this we simply leave out alternate scale tones as we ascend from the pitch of origin) yields the following family of diatonic chords, each of which is associated with the parallel diatonic mode. In the key of C, the diatonic *triads* (three-note chords) seen in example 1.5 result.

Example 1.5.

Extending this process to include a fourth note yields the diatonic *seventh* (four-note) chords (see example 1.6).

Example 1.6.

Although chords comprised of five, six, and seven notes are also possible, their inclusion at this point is not necesary.

Generically, then, we can obtain the intervallic descriptions for the diatonic triads and seventh chords in example 1.7.

Example 1.7.

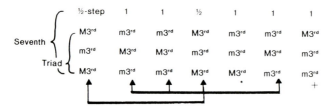

In discussing seventh chords, we refer to the note after which the chord is named as its *root,* and when this pitch is the lowest in a chord, as in the above examples, we refer to the chord as being in *root position.* Likewise, the second note up from the bottom in a root position chord is referred to as the *third* of the chord, the third note up is its *fifth,* and the highest note its *seventh.* Obviously, however, chords are not always voiced in root position. Chords, like individual intervals, may be inverted so that their individual pitches occur in any order. When such a process occurs so that the basic hierarchy of the voicing remains undisturbed, (for example, next up from the root is still the third, the fifth above that, and so on), the resulting chord is said to be in *inversion.* When the third of the chord becomes the lowest note in this procedure, the chord is said to be in *first inversion.* The fifth on the bottom produces what is known as *second inversion,* the seventh, *third inversion.* The diatonic seventh chords outlined above, then, each have four possible inversions, including root position. In example 1.8 they are accompanied by commonly used descriptive chord symbols and associated intervallic formulas.

Example 1.8.

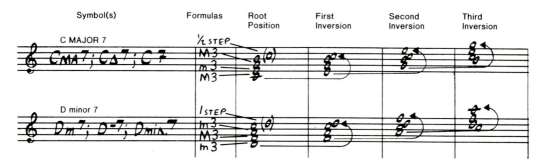

When the normal hierarchy of root, third, fifth, and seventh *is* disturbed in the creation of a new voicing for the chord, the result is known as an *open position* chord. These are especially common in vocal and instrumental music because the range in which each of the pitches is now distributed is wider and perhaps more comfortable for the individual voice or instrument assigned to each part. Example 1.9 demonstrates open voicings.

Example 1.9.

As was the case with the diatonic scales discussed earlier, other types of chords, although they are not diatonic, are used with enough frequency to warrant attention. These additional and important basic chord types and their formulas are listed in example 1.10.

intervals and scale and chord construction   9

Example 1.10.

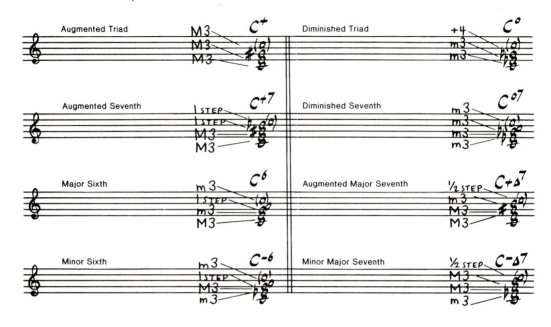

---

exercises

The following exercises provide reinforcement of the concepts presented in this chapter. In some cases (exercises 4, 5, and 8, for example) these provide good models for supplementary reference materials that you may wish to develop on your own. Only with a fluent understanding of these basic materials can we approach the concept of altering the coloration and richness of the various chord types we have discussed in order to make them sound more distinctively like jazz harmonies.

Exercise 1.1. Referring to table 1.3, label the following intervals:

Exercise 1.2. Identify the intervals played on the piano by your instructor (oral).

Exercise 1.3. Complete the transpositions of the given pairs of intervals as indicated:

Exercise 1.4. Write out the indicated related diatonic modes in the following keys (refer to table 1.4):

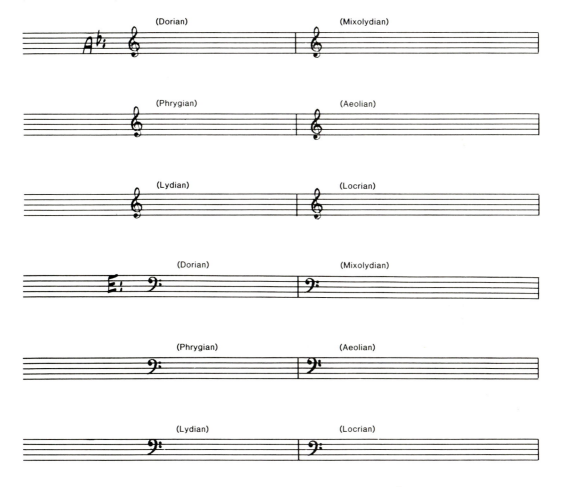

Exercise 1.5. Label the following modes (refer to Table 1.4; assume the left-most note is the root):

Exercise 1.6. Identify the modes played on the piano by your instructor (oral).

Exercise 1.7a. Transpose the following series of root position seventh chords up to a minor third into second inversion:

Exercise 1.7b. Transpose the original series of chords in 1.7a down a perfect fourth into first inversion:

Exercise 1.8. Write out the diatonic seventh chords in the keys indicated in third inversion.

Exercise 1.9. Identify the type and, if possible, the inversion of the following chords played by your instructor (oral).

---

bibliography for further study

Brandt, Carl, and Roemer, Clinton. **Standardized Chord Symbol Notation.** Sherman Oaks, CA: Roerick Music, 1976.

Clough, John. **Scales, Intervals, Keys and Triads: A Self-Instruction Program.** New York: W. W. Norton, 1964.

Haerle, Dan. **Scales for Jazz Improvisation.** Lebanon, IN: Studio/PR, 1975.

Harris, Brian. "An introduction to jazz harmony." **Canadian Musician** 1 (1979):53, 63.

La Barbera, Pat. "Diatonic 7th chords and modes." **Canadian Musician** 2 (1980):64.

Salvatore, Joseph. "Jazz Improvisation: Principles and Practices Relating to Harmonic and Scalic Resources." Ph.D. dissertation, Florida State University, 1970.

2 cadences and chord function

After you have learned how to identify and construct the basic chord types, the next step is to learn to combine them in various ways. A series of chords is known as a *chord progression*. Chords combine to form progressions in much the same way as atoms form molecules. And just as in chemistry, it is the further combination of these basic building blocks into larger units that results in more complex and readily identifiable structures regarded as so indispensable to our understanding of the musical world. Of all these combinations, some appear more frequently than others. The most commonly used combinations of chords are known as *cadences*. In a cadence, two or more chords progress to create an increased feeling of tension or harmonic instability followed by a return to a point of rest or harmonic stability. This perceived sense of stability or instability is created in our mind through a combination of everyday aural conditioning and actual acoustic phenomena. In any event, most harmonic movement in tonal music is perceived in terms of the degree to which the momentary harmony is gravitating toward or away from the most stable points within the key.

Two terms used to refer to the extremes of harmonic stability and instability within an individual chord or a chord progression are *dissonance* and *consonance*. Dissonance is the perception of harmonic or melodic instability, while consonance represents the opposite pole. It is of the utmost importance to bear in mind that these terms are relative in nature and should not be used in such a way as to imply value judgment. It is the context of each individual piece or musical event taken within the appropriate parameters of the value system of its own musical style that determines the relative dissonance or consonance within that style. To apply the strictures of one style in assessing music of another style is certainly not objective, and we must remember to take our own musical background, education, and cultural conditioning into account when assessing music that might not reflect these values. We should not assume that music that seems unduly dissonant to us is bad, but rather approach it with an appreciation for the fact that it reflects a different system of musical values in which a higher degree of what we label as dissonance may be a part. Our first impressions of such music will always be affected by our preconditioned concepts of what constitutes dissonance and consonance. Therefore, it is important to understand these basic intuitive reactions which so indelibly shape our ability to make sense of the music we hear in as objective a manner as possible. In short, it will simply not do to pass judgment on contemporary music using a value system to which an unexamined and antiquated concept of dissonance is fundamental.

The basic objective phenomena of tonal music reside in a few simple assumptions and definitions. By playing all of the diatonic chords in any order, we find that as Western listeners we have a strong desire to hear the dominant seventh of the key followed by the chord based on the root, or *tonic,* note of the key. Less strongly desired, but still satisfying to us, is a movement from the dominant chord to chords that contain many of the same pitches as the tonic chord. Aside from the dominant chord, diatonic chords built on the second and fourth degrees of the scale also tend to gravitate satisfactorily to our ears toward the tonic, although less strongly than does the dominant chord. In examining the construction of each of these groups of chords, we can see that they fall into the following functional categories according to whether or not they contain the fourth and/or seventh degrees of the scale. Note the addition of descriptive Roman numerals in table 2.1.

Table 2.1 .

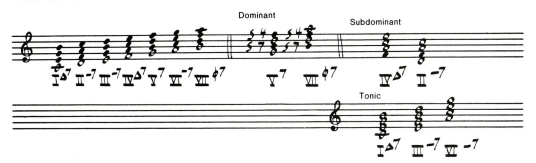

In jazz, we have three basic categories of functional harmony. *Dominant* chords (v7; VIIφ7) contain both the fourth and seventh degrees of the scale. *Subdominant* chords (II-7; IV MA7) contain only the fourth, and *tonic* chords do not contain the fourth degree of the scale. This differs from traditional harmony in which each diatonic chord has its own description (mediant, submediant, etc.). Thus while in jazz harmony the seventh degree of the scale is harmonically *stable* in the presence of a tonic chord, it is made quite dissonant in combination with the fourth scale degree, creating the dominant chord quality. The uniqueness of the interval occurring between these two unstable points in the scale creates the dissonance in example 2.1.

Example 2.1.

Bass motion also plays an important part in cadential activity. According to the style of music to which we are listening, certain of the different cadential possibilities may predominate and thereby in themselves constitute an important stylistic element. For example, cadential motion of IV-V in the bass suggests chorale-style harmony and creates the psychological expectation of music derivative of the classical style (see example 2.2).

Example 2.2.

The cadences of the seminal musical style of American art music, blues, were originally derived from church music. Consequently, this most basic of cadences found in Western tonal music also survives in rock music, a modern musical style not much advanced harmonically from blues. Cadential motion of *II-v,* on the other hand, suggests a more modern style in tonal music and is characteristic of relatively recent (post-1930) harmonic language in jazz and popular harmony.

Example 2.3.

Combined with other stylistic mannerisms of melody and rhythm, the type of bass motion we hear in a cadence may, therefore, be an important factor in determining the style of the music in question. Example 2.4 illustrates this point.

Example 2.4.

Of course, regardless of the dictates of the particular style of music under examination, variation in the form of harmonic deception is always possible. Example 2.5 deviates from the similar one just examined in its final chord, an intentional deception that depends for its success upon our expectation of the *former* bass motion.

Example 2.5.

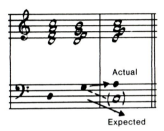

This is known as a *deceptive resolution*—a cadence that prepares the listeners for an obvious resolution and then surprises them with a different one.

As you know, Roman numerals are widely used in harmonic theory to describe chords within the diatonic system. Notice that in contemporary harmonic analysis we include the following elements in each Roman numeral description for a given chord: (1) *exact distance,* in the form of an abbreviated interval, from the tonic of the key to the root of the chord and (2) the chord's *type,* borrowed from the chord symbol. Because contemporary harmony often involves so much more complex harmonic relationships than does classical music, it is important that we adhere to absolutely specific descriptions for each chord. We cannot often assume strict diatonicism. The obvious advantage of Roman numerals is that they give us a more universal description of the functional relationships that create the particular chord progression, rather than simply naming it as a series of chords recognizable only in one key. Such an approach to harmonic analysis greatly facilitates such processes as transposition of particular chord progressions and identification of commonplace ones. Both skills are indispensable to a fluent use of harmonic materials.

From our previous definitions and common practice, the generalizations in table 2.2 concerning our perceptions of cadences might be drawn.

Table 2.2. Relative Strength of Cadences.

Weakest	———————	**Strongest**	
II–I	V–I	II–V–I	Jazz and Pop
IV–I	*VIIIϕ⁷–I	IV–V–I	Blues, Rock,
(SDM→T)	(D→T)	V–IV–I	Classical
*Rare			

We can generalize from our earlier observations regarding the functional grouping of the diatonic chords that chords which have many pitches in common may also share functional similarities. Such pitches are known as *common tones*. This intuitive observation is not always true, however. For example, we can easily see that while the chords D−7 and B♭ MA7 contain three common tones and therefore might both successfully harmonize many of the same melody notes, such an exchange would result in a change in harmonic function if this occurred in the key of F (see example 2.6). In other words, interchanging chords on the basis of common tones does not necessarily result in a progression that functions the same as the original one.

Example 2.6

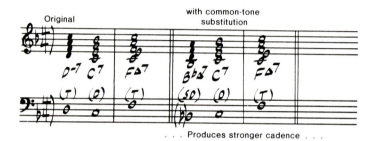

. . . Produces stronger cadence . . .

A final concept for this chapter is that while our harmonic system gradually expands to include many nondiatonic chords, the basic functional categories we have described here continue to shape our perceptions of cadences and the progression of chords.

exercises

Exercise 2.1. Name the subdominant chords in the key of F (oral).

Exercise 2.2. Name the tonic chords in the key of G♭ (oral).

Exercise 2.3. Name the dominant chords in the key of E (oral).

Exercise 2.4. Write out and label the subdominant chords in the following keys as indicated:

Exercise 2.5. Write out and label the tonic chords in the following keys as indicated:

Exercise 2.6. Write out and label the dominant chords in the following keys as indicated:

Exercise 2.7. Replace the indicated chords in each of the following cadences with one that would provide a stronger cadence (consult table 2.2). Be sure to label the new chords appropriately:

Exercise 2.8. Replace the indicated chords in each of the following short progressions with another chord of a *different* function that shares three common tones with it. Label these also:

Exercise 2.9. What are the following?

    a. VI-7 in the key of G
    b. VIIφ7 in the key of Ab
    c. II-7 in the key of B
    d. IV MA7 in the key of Db
    e. Subdominant chords in the key of A
    f. Dominant chords in the key of Ab

Exercise 2.10. Name two chords in the key of _____ that have three common tones yet different functions (oral).

bibliography for further study

Haerle, Dan. **Jazz Improvisation for Keyboard Players.** Lebanon, IN: Studio P/R, 1978.

Mehegan, John. "Tonal and Rhythmic Principles." **Jazz Improvisation.** New York: Watson-Guptill, 1959–1965.

Steedman, M. J. "The grammar of jazz chord sequences." **Bulletin of the British Psychological Society** (1979): 425.

Winkler, Peter. "Toward a theory of popular harmony." **In Theory Only** 4 (1978): 3–26.

Wolking, Henry. "Jazz theory and functional harmony." **NAJE Educator** 11 (1979): 82–83.

Wolking, Henry. "Jazz theory and functional harmony: part writing." **NAJE Educator** 11 (1980): 62–63.

Wolking, Henry. "Roots motion systems/major 3rd progressions." **NAJE Educator** 11 (1978/1979): 67–68.

voice-leading and embellishment

3

Now that you can identify and play chords and chord progressions to some extent, it becomes necessary to learn how to do so as smoothly and with as much variety and interest as possible. The two most basic concepts involved in these processes are voice-leading and embellishment. *Voice-leading* is defined as the most efficient motion possible from one chord voicing to the next. *Embellishment* is the process by which the voice-leading is decorated melodically without significantly altering its harmonic content.

   To illustrate the principle of voice-leading, example 3.1 demonstrates a chord progression in which each succeeding chord is voiced in root position, the common cadence in the key of C:

Example 3.1.

Clearly, there is very little efficiency in this movement between chords. Although occasionally a useful effect, this sort of parallelism does not make for very common or successful general practice. In order to voice-lead the same progression, simply apply the following principle: when moving from chord to chord, first identify any pitches that the adjacent chords have in common (these are called common tones). If there are any, hold them over, as demonstrated in example 3.2.

Example 3.2.

If there are no common tones, find the two notes in the adjacent chords that are closest to one another and keep them in the same voice. Next, move the remaining notes as dictated by the closest tones (see example 3.3).

Example 3.3.

When examining root motion between chords, we find that the following generalizations can be made with regard to voice-leading.

1. When the root motion is by any type of fourth or fifth, the third of the first chord moves to or becomes the seventh of the next, and vice-versa.

Example 3.4.

Similarly, the root of the first chord moves to the fifth of the next, and vice-versa.

Example 3.5.

In the more complex chord voicings to be studied later in this text, these same principles apply to anything *standing for* the root or the fifth of the chord in cases when they are replaced.

2. When the root motion is by any type of third or sixth, it is possible to voice-lead by means of retention of common tones.

Example 3.6.

It is also possible to voice-lead by finding the closest note between the adjacent voicings and treating it as if it were a common tone.

Example 3.7.

3. When the root motion is by any kind of a second or seventh, the following options may exist:
   a. *Common tone:*

Example 3.8.

   b. *Closest tone:*

Example 3.9.

   c. *Strict parallelism:*

Example 3.10.

Finally, there are voice-leading examples that are complicated by the presence of differing numbers of voices between adjacent chords. This necessitates a convergence or expansion of individual voices within the voice-leading. No rules exist for such situations other than using common sense and observing stepwise motion between as many of the inner parts as possible (see example 3.11).

Example 3.11.

Having tackled the mechanical problem of voice-leading, we now need to discuss the more musical problem of moving through a repeating chord progression with some sense of variety. There are many ways to generate interest as a given part of the progression recurs, and it is of equal value to the soloist as to the accompanist to bear them in mind. A first, simple method might be to begin the progression with a different inversion of the first chord each time, thereby necessitating a different approach to the subsequent voice-leading as illustrated in examples 3.12 and 3.13.

Example 3.12.

Example 3.13.

Sometimes, however, the use of particular inversions becomes impractical at a certain point due to considerations of range and muddiness. In order to avoid such situations without disturbing the smoothness of the voice-leading, it may be necessary to switch inversions. This should be done within the duration of an individual chord rather than between adjacent chords (examples 3.14 and 3.15).

Example 3.14.

muddy-low

Example 3.15.

solution

Another method of obtaining variety within the confines of a repeating chord progression is by *embellishing* it. The major problem to be confronted in this procedure is obviously the choice of notes to be used for this purpose. In general, these notes may be taken from the following sources:

    1. Notes may be *repeated* from elsewhere within the prior voice-leading of the same chord.

Example 3.16.

    2. Notes that may not be part of the seventh chord may sound good when played concurrently with it. These can be referred to as *tensions*, or *extensions*, of the chord and may or may not figure in the basic voice-leading of the chord themselves. They need not be diatonic (see chapter 5).

Example 3.17.

    3. Another source is notes that are not part of the seventh chord and that do *not* sound correct played with it. These might be referred to as *nonharmonic* or *passing tones*. They may occur in a variety of rhythmic contexts as long as they are not played in a manner that gives them undue harmonic stress. If a note falls into this category, it should *not* be:

a. *Leapt* from, except when followed immediately afterward by a melodic resolution, which is preferably chromatic

Example 3.18a.

b. Followed by a rest

Example 3.18b.

c. Allowed to last too long

Example 3.18c.

These same rules apply if the pitch in question constitutes a dissonance on the upcoming chord if this process is occurring at the actual point of chord change.

Example 3.19.

All of the above problems involving nonharmonic tones relate to the fact that our ear retains any pitch in its memory until its impression of that pitch is erased by the introduction of a neighboring tone or, in the case of a note followed by a rest, a certain passage of time. Charlie Parker, the father of modern jazz, is said to have put it best, "You're never more than a half step away from a right note."

Example 3.20 illustrates uses of all of the types of embellishment discussed above.

Example 3.20.

It can readily be seen that many successful embellishments employ arpeggiation heavily within the duration of the chord and then skillfully and correctly use increasingly dissonant passing tones to direct our ears toward the next significant point in the voice-leading to the upcoming chord. This is perhaps one reason why there is such a predominance of *blue notes* (see Ch. 11) in the melodies and accompaniments of the great jazz artists, as demonstrated in example 3.21.

Example 3.21.

When creating an embellishment of the voice-leading that is melodic, as opposed to harmonic, the player generally tries to bring out the most essential movement of an individual voice in that harmonic progression. Beyond the aesthetic decision involved in choosing which individual voice will become the melodic target of such an embellishment, its success also depends upon how well organized it is internally and how relevant stylistically it is to the composition. Several different versions of possible embellishments of a common chord progression follow. Analyze each for the following: (1) types of embellishment employed, (2) implied melodic target of the embellishment when voice-leading is continued to its logical conclusion in the next chord, and (3) internal organization.

Example 3.22a.

Example 3.22b.

Example 3.22c.

Example 3.22d.

What were the organizing principles that made some of the above examples sound different than the others? In general, this question can be answered by considering two basic guiding principles: (1) the relationship to the harmony and (2) the use of developmental techniques. Of course, the two principles may be combined.

Generally, every melody contains one or more main *motifs,* germs, or ideas. We readily identify these any time they are presented within the context of the piece based on their primary components. Every musical idea is given form by three basic elements: *rhythmic content, shape* (contour), and *harmonic implications.* We can refer to any combination of these three elements in improvising or writing over the course of the chord progression of the piece by using the following techniques of melodic development to create melody and/or to embellish the voice-leading:

1. Repeat the same melody or motivic fragment over different harmony or at a different point in the chord progression than where it originally occurred. As with all of the following techniques, chromatic or intervallic adjustments often need to be made to accommodate the change in harmony. This necessity rarely affects the musical effectiveness of the motif.

Example 3.23.

2. Repeat the same pattern (rhythmic, melodic, or harmonic) in any context. Several examples follow:
   a. Use of the same rhythmic pattern

Example 3.24a.

   b. Use of the same melodic pattern on different chords

Example 3.24b.

   c. Use of the same melodic pattern on the same chord

Example 3.24c.

   d. Repetition of a harmonic pattern
      (1) As a compositional device to help generate the structure of the piece itself

Example 3.25a.

      (2) Within a pre-existing chord progression

Example 3.25b.

e. Sequential repetition—a repetition of an idea at a different pitch level
(Some of the above examples may be regarded as sequential.)

Example 3.26.

3. Vary motifs. Although all of the above methods really present the same melodic fragment in different settings, it is possible to accomplish a variety of specific manipulations of the same small melodic germ or motif, with adjustments, where necessary, to accommodate the chord progression.
For example:

Example 3.27.

a. Retrograde—the same idea backwards

Example 3.28.

b. Inversion—the same idea upside down

Example 3.29.

c. Retrograde inversion—the same idea upside down and backwards (not necessarily repeated at the same pitch levels or with exact intervals)

Example 3.30.

d. Augmentation—the same idea with larger rhythmic values

Example 3.31.

e. Diminution—the same idea with smaller rhythmic values

Example 3.32.

f. Fragmentation—extracting one small part of an idea for any of the above purposes, or giving an otherwise concealed idea greater emphasis

Example 3.33.

g. Rhythmic displacement—using a melodic idea out of its original or traditional rhythmic context, usually changing the placement of the idea with respect to the placement of the accent of the meter

Example 3.34.

(The melodies of "Blue Monk" and "Straight, No Chaser" by Thelonious Monk contain excellent examples of rhythmic displacement.)

h. Elision—overlapping of two phrases so that the end of one melody is also the beginning of the next

Example 3.35.

The melody of "Giant Steps" by J. Coltrane (see appendix 1) contains an example of elision.

4. Replace an expected melodic resolution with a neighbor tone or dissonant note, thereby delaying the resolution in question (appoggiatura or indirect resolution). Example 3.36 demonstrates simple appoggiatura.

Example 3.36.

Many of these techniques might more commonly be associated with the European tradition of composition than with jazz. However, they are in evidence in the work of jazz artists through some combination of intellectual design and musical intuition which can be developed only through years of listening and playing. The following examples for analysis illustrate this:

Example 3.37.

Coltrane—*But Not For Me*

Example 3.37—Continued

Begin extended turnaround

Giant Steps

Example 3.37—Continued

Example 3.38.

McCoy Tyner's Solo on *"Bessie's Blues"*

Example 3.38—Continued

Example 3.39.

Clifford Brown—*Joyspring*

exercises

Exercise 3.1. Voice-lead the following chord progressions at the keyboard beginning with the inversion that is indicated. If it begins to sound "muddy," change inversions within the duration of one of the chords and then continue:

Exercise 3.2. Circle the nonharmonic tones in the following examples:

Exercise 3.3. Add passing tones to the following example where indicated:

Exercise 3.4. Given the following basic motif, describe the manipulations of it that have occurred in each example:

Exercise 3.5. Using the same motif, perform the indicated operations on it:

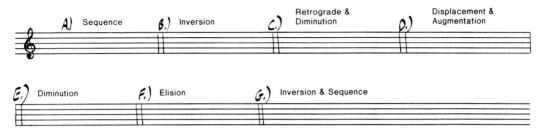

Exercise 3.6. Analyze and discuss the following excerpt from the point of view of the concepts of motivic development discussed in this chapter (see discography, chapter 10):

Donna Lee—*Charlie Parker*

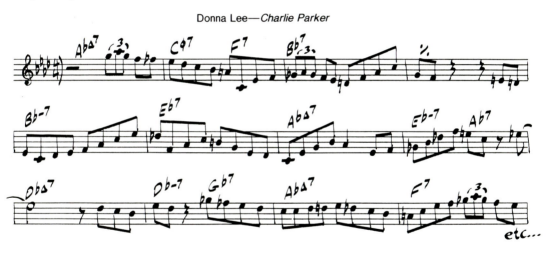

bibliography for further study

Aebersold, Jamey. **A New Approach to Improvisation.** New Albany, IN: Jamey Aebersold, 1980.

Alexander, Van. **The Be-bop Style.** New York: Criterion, 1949.

Armstrong, Louis. **Louis Armstrong's 44 Trumpet Solos and 125 Jazz Breaks.** New York: Edwin H. Morris & Co., Inc., 1951.

Baker, David. "Two classic Louis Armstrong solos." **Down Beat Music Handbook** (1977):66–67.

Blanq, Charles Clement. "Melodic Improvisation in American Jazz; the Style of Theodore 'Sonny' Rollins, 1951–1962." Ph.D. dissertation, Tulane University, 1977.

Carter, Ron. **Building a Jazz Bass Line.** New York: Ronald Carter Music, 1966–67.

Christian, Charlie. **Jazz Improvisation Transcriptions.** Tokyo: Nochion, Inc., 1975.

"Clark Terry's improvised solo on 'Straight No Chaser'. " **NAJE Educator** 10 (1978):38–39.

Hyman, Dick. "Those Tatum runs: a look at the great jazz pianist's solo style." **Contemporary Keyboard** 6 (1980): 6–7.

John Coltrane Jazz Improvisation Transcriptions. 2 vols. Tokyo: Nochion Inc., 1975.

Madsen, Jens Westergaard. "Bill Evans' harmonik: en praktisk test på nogle ideer; John Mehegans Jazz Imporvisation, bd. IV," **Musik & Forskning** 3 (1977): 129–140.

Nelson, Oliver. **Patterns for Jazz.** Hollywood, CA: Noslen Music, 1966.

Owens, Thomas. "Charlie Parker: Techniques of Improvisation." 2 vols. Ph.D. dissertation, University of California at Los Angeles, 1974.

Parker, Charlie. **Be-bop for Alto Sax.** New York: Atlantic Music Corp., 1948.

Charlie Parker Jazz Improvisation Transcriptions. Tokyo: Nochion, Inc., 1975.

Reid, Rufus. **The Evolving Bassist.** Chicago: Myriad Limited, 1974.

Ricker, Ramon. **New Concepts in Linear Improvisation.** Lebanon, IN: Studio P/R, 1977.

Rohm, Joseph W. "Jazz Harmony: Structure, Voicing, and Progression." Ph.D. dissertation, Florida State University, 1974.

Stewart, Milton. "Some characteristics of Clifford Brown's improvisational style." **Jazzforschung/Jazz Research** 11 (1979): 135–164.

Stewart, Milton. "Structural Development in the Jazz Improvisational Technique of Clifford Brown." Ph.D. dissertation, University of Michigan, 1973.

Taylor, Billy. "Jazz improvisation: melodic invention." **Contemporary Keyboard** 6 (1980): 82.

———. "Jazz improvisation part 2: harmonic resources." **Contemporary Keyboard** 6 (1980): 53.

———. "Jazz improvisation part 3: rhythmic devices." **Contemporary Keyboard** 6 (1980): 67.

White, Andrew. **The Works of John Coltrane.** 10 vols. Washington, D.C.: Andrew's Musical Enterprises, n.d.

discography for further study

"Bessie's Blues." **The Best of John Coltrane.** Impulse AS 9200.
"But Not For Me." **My Favorite Things.** Atlantic SD 1361.
"Joyspring." **Daahoud.** Mainstream MRL 386.

4 secondary dominants

We now discuss specific categories of nondiatonic chords in common use in the context of primarily diatonic progressions. *Nondiatonic chords* are those that include one or more pitches foreign to the key in which they operate, as in example 4.1.

Example 4.1.

While there are several important functional groups of nondiatonic chords that together have the overall effect of expanding the scope of the diatonic system, none is more important or more commonly used than the secondary dominants. *Secondary dominant* sevenths are those dominant sevenths built on the first, second, third, sixth, and seventh degrees of the diatonic scale.

Example 4.2.

We expect them to resolve to the diatonic chords whose roots are found a perfect fifth below. Therefore, just as we expect the primary dominant seventh found diatonically in the key to resolve down a fifth to the tonic chord, we anticipate that the five secondary dominant sevenths related to the key will do likewise, each with its own presumed target.

Example 4.3.

While a dominant seventh built on the fourth degree of the scale also occurs frequently, it is not a secondary dominant, since there is no diatonic target chord available for it to resolve to. Further, no secondary dominant is available for the diatonic seventh chord built on the seventh degree (VIIø 7), since there is no diatonic scale degree available to serve as the root of such a secondary dominant.

Example 4.4.

Secondary dominants are effective for two reasons: first, they are nondiatonic and catch our attention because they temporarily disturb our sense of tonality; second, when they resolve, they have the effect of temporarily strengthening the importance of the diatonic chord to which they do resolve. In the context of a bass motion that remains diatonic they allow the introduction of nondiatonic harmony. This, in turn, creates not just the simple motion from one diatonic chord to another, but an actual sense of resolution to a particular diatonic chord, thereby attaching more importance and interest to it. Consider this concept in comparing the two progressions in examples 4.5a and 4.5b.

Example 4.5a.

Example 4.5b.

Dominant seventh chords (see chapter 2) contain the interval of an augmented fourth, or *tritone*, between their third and seventh. This also represents the interval between the fourth and seventh scale degrees of the key whose root lies a perfect fifth lower. This relationship exists whether one discusses major or minor key harmony (see examples 4.6a and 4.6b).

Example 4.6a.

Example 4.6b.

It is the presence of this tritone in the dominant seventh chord of a given key, and its uniqueness within the diatonic system, that creates the strong desire in our ear for resolution of the dominant seventh chord (see Ch. 2). The fact that the root of a dominant seventh chord is as far away as possible from the tonic of the key makes this desire even stronger. Thus, placing a dominant seventh a fifth above a given diatonic chord, in lieu of another diatonic chord that does not contain a tritone, yields the temporary sense of tonality to the target diatonic chord. We expect the tritone of such a dominant seventh chord to resolve to the root and third of its diatonic target chord in exactly the same way as the primary dominant seventh chord of the key resolves to the tonic chord in the primary key.

Example 4.7a.

Example 4.7b.

This process is known as *tonicization.* The diatonic target chord that a secondary dominant seventh chord presumes is known as the tonic chord of a *key-of-the-moment,* or *temporary key.* Thus, the secondary dominant built on the second scale degree is called V7/V, and its presence implies the key-of-the-moment of V.

Example 4.8.

Since we hear all tonal music in relation to a major or minor key, the quality (major or minor) of the diatonic triad that assumes the role of the temporary tonic chord determines the quality of the temporary key. Thus, V7/V and IV are major keys-of-the-moment, while V7/II, III and VI are minor keys-of-the-moment, as seen in example 4.9.

Example 4.9.

This is another reason why there is no practical secondary dominant for the target chord VIIø. The diatonic triad on the seventh scale degree is diminished and would not constitute an adequately stable tonic chord, even temporarily.

Secondary dominant sevenths and their related keys-of-the-moment differ from actual *modulations* (see chapter 9) in that they always continue in the original key following the resolution of the given secondary dominant. They strengthen tonality by attaching greater importance to diatonic chords, but do not change it (see example 4.10).

Example 4.10.

As with any dominant chord, secondary dominants need not actually resolve to the temporary key they imply. Thus, a deceptive resolution of a secondary dominant seventh chord involves a chord progression where *anything other than* the expected diatonic target follows the secondary dominant. In most such cases the musician or composer plays or writes on the secondary dominant as if it were actually going to resolve normally, thus heightening the effect of the deception. Three basic categories of deceptive resolutions exist for secondary dominants.

   1. The secondary dominant is *preceded* by the *tonic* chord of the key and *returns to it* rather than to its expected diatonic target chord (see chapter 7).

Example 4.11a.

Good examples of this are the tunes, "Meditation" by A. C. Jobim and "Groovin' High" by Dizzy Gillespie. These tunes involve a back-and-forth motion between the tonic chord and V7/III (see chapter 7).

2. A chord with the *expected diatonic root* follows the secondary dominant, but a chord of a *different quality* is built upon that root.

Example 4.11b.

3. A chord that *substitutes* for the expected diatonic target chord follows the secondary dominant, either due to common tones between the two interchanged chords or due to similarity of function (see chapter 6).

Example 4.11ci.

Example 4.11cii.

A special subset, the *extended dominant,* evolves from this last group. Extended dominants may begin with what sounds like a traditional secondary dominant. This secondary dominant then resolves deceptively to a chord with the expected diatonic root but that is dominant in quality. This dominant seventh then, in turn, resolves to yet another dominant seventh, and so on. In an extended dominant situation, our ear eventually expects the dominant chords involved to resolve to other dominant chords rather than to normally expected diatonic targets. This happens even though each of the chords in the progression might also have a potential secondary dominant function within the key if it were encountered under other circumstances. In extended dominant situations, it is most common to treat keys-of-the-moment as major, since this is the quality of the triad contained within the dominant seventh chord (see example 4.12).

Example 4.12.

In minor keys-of-the-moment, we have an additional problem of deciding which form of minor (see chapter 6) we should use to best establish the quality of the temporary key. This is part of the larger question of scales for use in association with secondary dominants.

All chords can be thought of as derived from or related to particular scales. The passing tones within the scale with which a particular chord is associated fall into two categories: (1) those that are consonant with the chord and constitute points of stability in addition to the chord tones themselves (known as *tensions* or *extensions* of the chord), and (2) those that are dissonant with the chord and must be treated strictly as passing or nonharmonic tones (see chapter 3). The number of tensions, as opposed to dissonances within a particular scale, depends upon the manner in which the scale for a particular chord was derived as well as upon the type of chord under consideration. For example, where diatonic chords are concerned, the scale associated with them is generally thought to be the diatonic scale itself, starting on the root of the chord. Thus, a II-7 chord contains no dissonance within its associated scale, while III-7 contains two.

Example 4.13.

G-7; II-7; F Major from G°G = g-Dorian   A-7; III-7; F Major from A-A = A-Phrygian

In general, our ear identifies the following types of pitches as being dissonant with regard to particular types of chords:

    1. Nondominant chords—any pitch a half step above a chord tone

Example 4.14a.

Example 4.14b.

Example 4.14c.

F⁻⁷

2. Dominant chord—any pitch a half step above the third or seventh

Example 4.14d.

C⁷

Example 4.14e.

A♭⁷

As a result of these considerations, two different philosophies of constructing scales for particular chords evolved. The first, and the earliest, says that any diatonic chord employs that diatonic scale from which it has been derived and that any nondiatonic chord used in a particular key must derive all of its passing tones diatonically.

Example 4.15a.

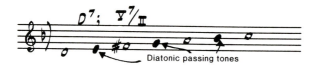

Diatonic passing tones

Example 4.15b.

Diatonic passing tones

The second, and more recent, procedure states that the choice between alternative scales should be the scale that contains the maximum amount of consonance, the scale that *minimizes* the number of nonharmonic tones in the scale. Thus, the scale containing the most tensions (least dissonance) is chosen by considering the particular type of chord, rather than by considering the function of a chord at a particular juncture. According to this philosophy, certain scales become *generically* associated with particular types of chords (see Appendix 6). Under this system, for example, all minor seventh chords use the dorian scale, regardless of their function in a particular key, since it maximizes tension and minimizes dissonance when compared to other minor seventh scales.

Example 4.16.

While this topic will be discussed in greater detail later, it is easy to see its relevance to the discussion of the secondary dominant question. For each secondary dominant seventh, we have two choices. One is to spell the chord and fill in the spaces between chord tones with diatonic passing tones until we have one version of each pitch in the scale.

Example 4.17a.

The other choice is to fill these spaces with other points of consonance of our choosing, thus achieving a variety of possibilities, for example.

Example 4.17b.

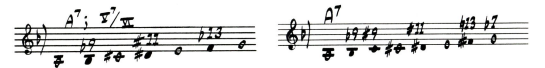

In experimenting with these possibilities, you will come to your own conclusions regarding the validity and attractiveness of the sound of each of the scales you derive. Bearing in mind the intended function of particular secondary dominants vis-a-vis their presumed use in embellishing our broader sense of the tonality, you can begin to hear the need to differentiate between those tensions associated with expected major temporary keys and those involving temporary minor keys. In so doing, you find that where the implied target chord is of a minor quality, the related secondary dominant should have the tension ♭13. (Tensions, like compound intervals (see chapter 1) derive their nomenclature from adding the degree of the scale they represent to 7. Bear in mind that a tension is a consonant point in a scale other than a chord tone *in the presence of a seventh chord*.) This is because the same pitch that is ♭13 on a dominant seventh is the *minor* third of the diatonic target chord.

Example 4.18.

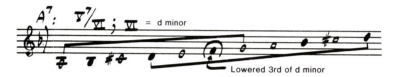

Conversely, the presence of *natural 13* in a dominant seventh chord's scale presumes the presence of *major* quality target chord.

Example 4.19.

The only remaining questions concern the quality of the scale tones that intervene between the root and third of a chord and between the third and the fifth. In most key-of-the-moment situations, it is advisable to include the root of the key-of-the-moment in the scale used for the related dominant. This note will be the eleventh of the chord, and it is dissonant on any dominant chord since it will inevitably be found a half step above the third of the chord (see Examples 4.14).

Example 4.20.

Thus, the root of the key or key-of-the-moment, if it is retained in the scale of the related dominant or secondary dominant chord, is a nonharmonic tone and must be treated accordingly (see chapter 3).

This leaves only the quality of the ninth to determine, and as it turns out, either ♭9 or natural 9 seems to move equally well to major or minor target chords. In order to simplify matters for the moment, let us assume that ♭9 is associated with V7/II,

III, and VI, while natural nine is associated with V7/V and IV. In making this basic assumption, we find, when combining this idea with the previous determinations made about the ninth and thirteenth, that the following distinctions can be made:

1. Dominant seventh chords in *major keys-of-the-moment* (V7/IV, V, I, and extended dominants) use the *major scale* of the *temporary target chord* starting on the root of the given dominant. In other words, G7 uses the C major scale starting on G. This, of course, yields the mixolydian mode (see chapter 1).

Example 4.21.

2. Dominant seventh chords in *minor keys-of-the-moment* (V7/II, III, and VI) use the *harmonic minor scale* based on the root of the *diatonic target chord,* starting on the root of the related dominant. In other words, G7 uses the C harmonic minor scale starting on G.

Example 4.22.

Comparing the two scales in examples 4.21 and 4.22 with the scales obtained by simply arpeggiating the secondary dominant and filling in diatonic passing tones shows their similarity. V7/II is an exception, and has a natural nine rather than a ♭9. This of course simply means that we have derived a *melodic,* rather than harmonic, minor key-of-the-moment (see chapter 1).

Example 4.23.

In actual practice, the scale shown in example 4.23 is less commonly used on V7/II than the harmonic minor from the fifth scale.

To summarize, secondary dominant seventh chords set up the implied resolution to a major or minor temporary key depending on the quality of their diatonic target triad. Those that establish the minor quality key-of-the-moment always contain ♭13, and generally ♭9 also, while the presence of natural tensions conversely creates the expectation for resolution to a major quality chord. Remember also that even when a deceptive resolution is anticipated, these considerations contribute to heightening its effect.

Example 4.24 combines these principles with the concepts of embellishment discussed in chapter 3. It moves from an unembellished chord progression, through a step-by-step process that leads to the use of appropriate tensions and dissonant passing tones to a point where every note in the chromatic scale has been used melodically without obscuring the direction of the chord progression.

Example 4.24a.

Example 4.24b.

Example 4.24c.

Example 4.24d.

Table 4.1 shows the extensions of the diatonic system made possible by the inclusion in the system of secondary dominants.

Table 4.1.

Key of F:	FMA⁷	G⁻⁷	A⁻⁷	BbΔ⁷	C⁷	D⁻⁷	E⁻ϕ⁷
	IΔ⁷	II⁻⁷	III⁻⁷	IVΔ⁷	V⁷	VI⁻⁷	VIIϕ⁷

Secondary dominant	—		D⁷	E⁷	F⁷	G⁷	A⁷	—
			V⁷/II	V⁷/III	V⁷/IV	V⁷/V	V⁷/VI	

There is yet one more simple process that may occur in relation to secondary dominants. Unless melodic considerations make it impossible, any secondary dominant may be preceded by its *related minor seventh* (meaning the minor seventh whose root is a fourth lower). In other words, if a given dominant seventh is functioning in a given key or key-of-the-moment, its cadential effect can be made even greater by making it part of a more complete cadence (see chapter 2). *Interpolating* the related II-7 in a major key-of-the-moment or the related IIϕ7 in a minor key-of-the moment will do the trick. Scales associated with these chords are dorian and locrian, respectively, the major scale or natural minor scales of the key-of-the-moment beginning on the *second* degree.

Example 4.25a.

Example 4.25b.

Although the secondary dominant chord uses the harmonic minor scale from the fifth degree in minor keys-of-the-moment, the practice on the related IIϕ7 has been to use the *natural minor* scale from the second degree. Apparently, the locrian mode has become the generic scale for IIϕ sevenths because, compared with the harmonic minor scale from the second degree, it contains tension ♭13, which is indigenous among minor quality chords to the ϕ7.

Example 4.26.

The chords in examples 4.25a and 4.25b could further expand table 4.1 were they to be included in it. Please note that some of these related cadential minor seventh or minor seven flat five chords are also diatonic to the primary key, while others are not.

Table 4.2.

Diatonic Harmony (Key of F)	FΔ⁷ (IΔ⁷)	G⁻⁷ (II⁻⁷)	A⁻⁷ (III⁻⁷)	BbΔ⁷ (IVΔ⁷)	C⁷ (V⁷)	D⁻⁷ (VI⁻⁷)	Eø⁷ (VIIø⁷)
Secondary dominant 7th	None	D⁷ (V⁷/II)	E⁷ (V⁷/III)	F⁷ (V⁷/IV)	G⁷ (V⁷/V)	A⁷ (V⁷/VI)	None
Related cadential ⁻7		A⁻⁷ (III⁻⁷)	B⁻⁷ (*)	C⁻⁷ (*)	D⁻⁷ (VI⁻⁷)	E⁻⁷ (*)	

*Nondiatonic related ⁻⁷.

The tune "Meditation," referred to earlier, constitutes a good example of this principle.

Example 4.27.

---

exercises

Exercise 4.1.   List the secondary dominant sevenths in the given
keys: Bb: V7/II____   V7/III____   V7/IV____   V7/V____   V7/VI____
            E: V7/II____   V7/III____   V7/IV____   V7/V____   V7/VI____

Exercise 4.2.   The following chords would be V7/II in what keys?
            C7____   Eb7____   A7____   Db7____
            The following chords would be V7/IV in what keys?
            Gb7____   A7____   D7____   Cb7____

Exercise 4.3. Label each of the following chords with both a chord symbol *and* a roman numeral; then supply the correct target chord:

Exercise 4.4. Create scales for the following secondary dominants by filling in their arpeggios with diatonic passing tones:

Exercise 4.5. List those pitches on the given chords that will automatically be dissonant (consult example 4.14):

Exercise 4.6. Add related minor seven or ∅7 chords to the following chord progression as indicated. Supply the appropriate scales as well (consult example 4.25):

Exercise 4.7. Thoroughly analyze and discuss the following example from the point of view of both melodic and harmonic practices discussed in the last two chapters (see discography, chapter 7):

"Groovin' High"—D. Gillespie

Exercise 4.7—Continued

bibliography for further study

Mehegan, John. **Studies in Jazz Harmony.** New York: Sam Fox, 1972.

Taylor, Billy. "Jazz improvisation part 2: harmonic resources." **Contemporary Keyboard** 6 (1980): 53.

common chord progressions

5

This chapter explains commonplace chord progressions. You should become familiar enough with these to be able to voice-lead them and identify them aurally. Learn these basic progressions in several keys and become familiar with the standard tunes listed as being representative of each. For improvisation or writing on these basic progressions, try to develop a conception that does not rely too heavily on scales as a source of material for improvisation. As your knowledge of theory improves, you may incorporate chord-scale/chord-substitution concepts into your playing. However, greater dependence on your ear, rather than on a set of intellectually grounded concepts, will be to your advantage now. Forcing yourself to rely on your ear will improve your aural skills. Play basic voice-led arpeggiation of these progressions, connecting chord tones by passing tones of your choice. When a note seems unstable on a chord, treat it as you would any passing note, not emphasizing it too much rhythmically. Another valuable concept when beginning improvisation is to arrive at a set of available notes for a given chord by creating a scale made of the basic chord tones of the seventh chord with passing tones derived diatonically from the key or key-of-the-moment in which the chord is functioning. Many of the following simple progressions are followed by a list of standard and jazz tunes that contain the particular progression. The importance of being able to recognize and play over these basic harmonic building blocks of jazz cannot be overemphasized.

The first group consists of common turnarounds—repeating progressions of three or four chords usually ending on an unresolved dominant seventh or other cadence. These serve as the basis for many improvised endings and introductions and become a part of the actual progressions of many tunes (table 5.1).

Table 5.1. Common Turnarounds.

Characteristics

(A) I VI⁻⁷ II⁻⁷ V⁷

Diatonic

(B) II⁻⁷ V⁻⁷ I⁻⁷ V⁷

Diatonic beginning on 3rd

Table 5.1—*Continued*

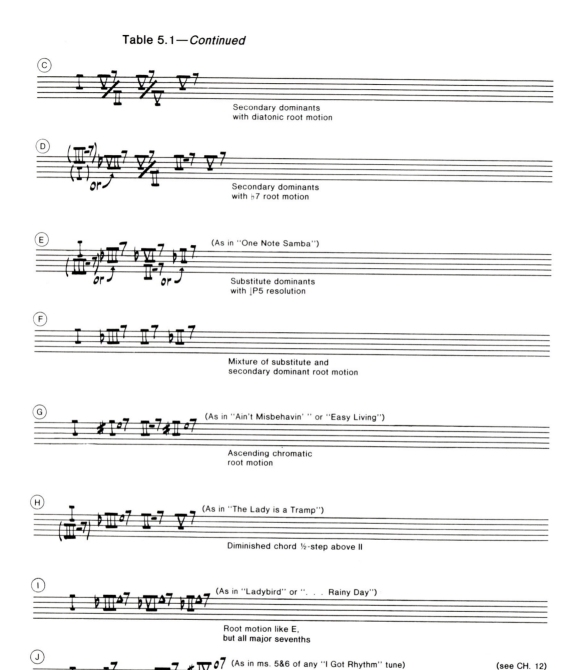

60   common chord progressions

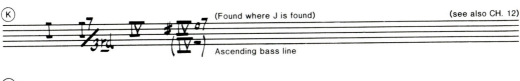

The second group of common progressions involves the basic twelve-bar blues progression (see chapter 10) and its many variations (table 5.2).

Table 5.2. Common Blues Progressions.

*See page 69.

Table 5.2—*Continued*

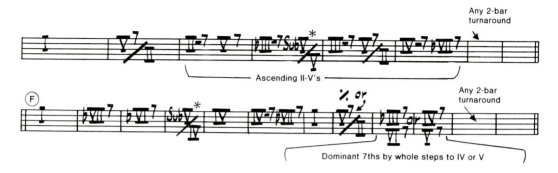

The third group involves common relationships between *two-fives* (table 5.3).

Table 5.3. Two-Fives.

*See page 69.

The progressions listed above undergo many permutations and recombinations to create even more possibilities. While this is by no means an exhaustive list of the chord progressions you will encounter in jazz harmony, it is one that creates the basis for developing your aural skills further as you learn to hear more complex and sophisticated harmonic relationships.

Exercises

Exercise 5.1. Identify the following short progressions played on the piano by your instructor (oral):

Exercise 5.2. Write down the simple blues chord progressions played at the piano by your instructor:

Exercise 5.3a, 5.3b. Write out a solo to the following chord progressions by voice-leading the indicated chord progression and linking chord tones by nonharmonic tones chosen from the key or key-of-the-moment:

bibliography for further study

Baker, David. **Techniques of Improvisation.** Chicago: Maher Publications, 1971.

Markewich, Reese. **The New Expanded Bibliography of Jazz Compositions Based on the Chord Progressions of Standard Tunes.** Pleasantville, NY: Markewich, 1974.

Pyke, Launcelot A. "Jazz, 1920–1927: An Analytical Study." 2 vols. Ph.D. dissertation, University of Iowa, 1962.

Roberts, Howard. "Jazz improvisation: creating chord progressions." **Guitar Player** 14 (1980): 101, 102, 110.

Taylor, Billy. "Jazz improvisation: learning to improvise part 1: introductions." **Contemporary Keyboard** 6 (1980): 68.

————. "Jazz improvisation: learning to improvise part 2: interludes." **Contemporary Keyboard** 6 (1980): 57, 65.

Wolking, Henry. "Root motion systems / major 3rd progressions." **NAJE Educator** 11 (1978 / 1979): 67–68.

discography for further study

"Afternoon in Paris." **Modern Jazz Quartet At the Music Inn.** Atlantic S-1299

"Ain't Misbehavin'." **Ain't Misbehavin',** Fats Waller. Everest Records #EVR 5337.

"Angel Eyes." **John Coltrane With Johnny Hartman.** Impulse 40.

"Au Privave." **Return Engagement.** MGM V3HB-8840.

"Blue Bossa." **Joe Henderson Page One.** Blue Note 84140.

"Bluesette." **Together Again for the First Time.** Gryphon G 903.

"Blues For Alice." **Swedish Schnapps.** Verve 68010.

"Ceora." **Lee Morgan Memorial Album.** Blue Note LA 224-G.

"Confirmation." **Return Engagement.** MGM V3HB-8840.

"Easy Livin'." **Bouncin' With Dex,** Dexter Gordon. Inner City Records #2060.

"Here's That Rainy Day." **Straight Life.** CTI 6007.

"Joyspring." **Daahoud.** Mainstream MRL 386.

"Mean to Me." **Ain't Nobody's Business If I Do.** Columbia P4 12969.

"One Note Samba." **Terra Brasilis.** Warner Brothers 28 3409.

"Ornithology." **Charlie Parker on Dial, Vol. 1.** Spotlight 101.

"Satin Doll." **Ellingtonia, Vol. 2.** 2-Impulse 9285.

"The Lady Is a Tramp." **Basie's Thing,** Count Basie. EMI Records #S154D-99436.

"Till There Was You." **Meet the Beatles.** Capitol ST 2047.

"What's New." **Ballads,** John Coltrane. Impulse A32 / AS32.

substitute dominants and dominant seventh chord scales

6

Before embarking on a theoretical discussion of dominant seventh chord scales, it is useful to adopt a set of generalizations concerning possible combinations of pitches within these scales. Consult appendix 6 frequently in conjunction with this chapter.

First, all of the dominant seventh scales discussed in this chapter contain their tonic, third, and sevenths, since these are the pitches that define the chord's quality.

Example 6.1.

Further, all dominant seventh chord scales fall into one of two general categories: scales that are *mixolydian related* and those that are not. Mixolydian-related scales always contain a *fourth* and a *fifth* degree. The fourth scale degree of a mixolydian scale is significant because it is the tonic of the key or key-of-the-moment in which the associated dominant seventh chord operates. Although the fourth degree is the tonic of the target chord of the dominant seventh chord, it should not be stressed melodically during the duration of the dominant seventh chord. It is a half step above the *third* of the chord with which it would conflict melodically (see p. 51). Thus, dominant seventh scales containing a *fourth* scale degree also contain a *fifth* scale degree (although not necessarily vice versa). Example 6.2 illustrates the different forms mixolydian scales may take. Note that *all* of these have the tones 1, 3, 4, 5, and ♭7 in common.

Example 6.2.

Between the tonic and the third of the scale occurs the *ninth* of the scale. Ninths are either *altered* or *natural* (or *diatonic*). The presence of a natural ninth in a scale precludes the possibility of an altered ninth in that scale, and vice versa. Likewise, the presence of *either* a ♭9 or a ♯9 in a scale implies the *coexistence* in that scale of the other, and vice versa. Therefore, the lower tetrachord of a dominant seventh scale (see previous examples) may take either of the two basic forms which follow in example 6.3.

Example 6.3.

The next portion of the scale is that region between the third and the seventh. As our previous mixolydian variants showed us, an unaltered fourth scale degree implies the presence of an unaltered fifth scale degree as well (see previous examples). The reverse is not necessarily true, however. The following two scales are no longer mixolydian due precisely to the *replacement* of the fourth degree of the scale with a *raised* fourth, yet they still contain a fifth scale degree in the unaltered form. Notice that the combination of ♯4 and natural 5 in a dominant seventh scale implies an upper tetrachord which then continues: ♯4,5,6(13),♭7, and 1.

Example 6.4.

A final group of nonmixolydian scales features the replacement of the natural fourth and fifth scale degrees with *flatted* fifth and sixth scale degrees respectively, yielding the altered upper tetrachord, producing a scale, which, unlike those just examined, no longer contains a fourth degree.

Example 6.5.

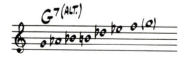

Table 6.1 summarizes the relationships detailed to this point.

Table 6.1. Dominant Scale Forms.

Scale	Name/Characteristics
G Mixolydian	♮4, ♮5, ♮9, ♮13
G Lydian ♭7	♯11, ♮5, ♮9, ♮13
G Mixolydian ♭9 (C "harmonic major" from 5th)	♭9(♯9), ♮4, ♮5, ♮13
G Altered (contains no 4th degree)	♭9(♯9), ♭5, ♭13
G Mixolydian ♭9, ♭13 (C harmonic minor from 5th)	♭9(♯9), ♭13, ♮4, ♮5
G Mixolydian ♭13 (C melodic minor from 5th)	♮4, ♮5, ♮9, ♭13
G Whole-tone	♯11, ♭13
G ½,1-step symmetric diminished	♭9(♯9), ♯11, ♮5, ♮13

Having established these generalities regarding dominant seventh chord scale construction, let us examine their origin in more theoretical terms.

Substitute dominants are dominant seventh chords that replace V7 or any of the standard secondary dominants in a key. The cause of that replacement is functional similarity, based on the *shared tritone*. Look at the dominant chord in the key of C, G7 in example 6.6.

Example 6.6.

The chord quality of a dominant seventh is expressed in its *tritone;* in the case of G7 the notes are B and F. The principle of dominant seventh chord substitution simply says that dominant chords sharing this same tritone are functional substitutes. Conveniently, these chords are found in pairs with roots an augmented fourth (or tritone) apart. Thus, the definition of dominant seventh chord substitution includes two different meanings of the term tritone. It could best be summarized as follows: dominant seventh chords with roots a *tritone* (augmented fourth) apart share the same *tritone* (third and seventh) and are functional substitutes for one another. This in turn implies that resolution of either chord could occur to either of two common destinations—one of which would be the traditional fifth below, the other one-half step lower.

Example 6.7.

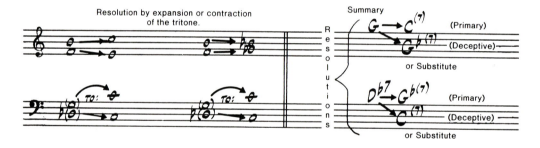

Since the most conventional of jazz cadences has the root motion II-V-I, it is easy to understand how this substitution evolved.

Example 6.8.

In step 2.) the approach notes in the bass create the busier harmonic rhythm
associated with evolution of more modern Jazz styles.

The generally accepted terminology regarding these chords is that the D♭7 be regarded as the *substitute* for the G7 and, just as the G7 is called V7 *of* I, so the D♭7 becomes known as "SubV of I." Therefore, substitute dominants exist a tritone (distance) apart, share the same tritone (chord quality), and when one is "V of X" in a given key, its substitute is called "Sub V of X" in that key, and vice versa. The *substitute* dominant occurs a half step above its implied target, just as the dominant of a given chord occurs a fifth above. In addition to secondary dominants, then, we have the substitute dominants in example 6.9 available to expand upon the diatonic system.

Example 6.9.

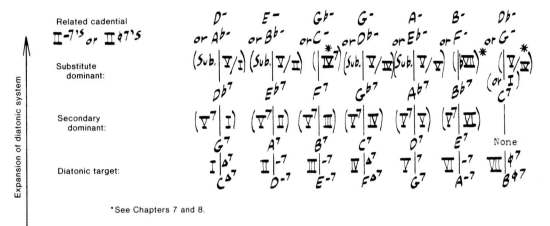

*See Chapters 7 and 8.

Notice that no provision has been made for a "Sub V of III (or) VII." Although any dominant chord may resolve downward by a half step after the fashion of a substitute dominant, this does not necessarily mean that our ears perceive that motion as a substitute harmonic activity. Dominant chords that move down one half step to III or VII chords are of course known as IV7 and I7, respectively, since they most commonly function in this manner in blues harmony (see chapters 7 and 9). They may resolve downward by a half step, but when this occurs, it constitutes a deception to our conditioning as jazz listeners.

Example 6.10.

What about secondary or extended dominants resolving down by half steps? Are they considered substitute dominants because they have adopted their function? No. Most theorists acknowledge a *primary function* for every dominant chord within a given key. Any other resolution (or the lack of it) constitutes some sort of a deception of our ears. This does not change the primary function of that chord within the key or its analysis, however, since any deceptive resolution depends mostly on comparison with that "normal" function of the given chord. Any change in the analysis or melodic treatment of a particular chord for the sake of reflecting its ultimate destination might, in fact, work towards giving that move away, thereby depriving it of some of its musical effect. In other words, one usually treats a dominant chord as if it were going where it was expected to go within the key, even if one knows better.

What about the chord scales generally associated with dominant seventh chords and their substitutes? What effect does the new substitute root motion have on the hierarchy of the original chord tones and tensions in relation to this new bass note? To obtain the answers to both questions, we can examine a few voicings that reflect the various possible combinations of ninths and thirteenths within dominant seventh structures for the effect of displacement of the root by the distance of a tritone. We can then apply our rules regarding placement of tensions within a scale.

First of all, let us start with the scale that generated V7/I, the mixolydian mode, illustrated in example 6.11.

Example 6.11.

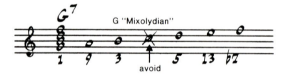

Notice that it implies natural 9 and 13 as tensions, and that the eleventh is avoided because it creates a half step above the third of the chord. This problem can be averted by incorporating the root of the substitute dominant seventh (in this case Db7) into the scale. It replaces the tonic of the key (in this case C) in the scale.

Example 6.12.

Now the V7 chord has not only diatonic tensions 9 and 13, but an additional available tension, ♯11. The resulting scale can be employed anywhere a mixolydian scale would ordinarily be used, as long as the fifth of the chord does not appear in the melody, with which the new tension, ♯11, would clash.

Example 6.13.

If we examine the scale in Example 6.12., we see that it follows our previously established rules regarding the coexistence of tensions within a scale. This is known as the *lydian ♭7* scale, and you should become as familiar with its interval structure as with the other major, minor, and modal scales previously discussed. Displacement of the root of this scale to the tritone substitute yields a dominant seventh chord scale with *altered* tensions. This also follows our previously established rules regarding the coexistence of tensions within the same scale. This scale is known as the *altered* or *superlocrian* scale.

Example 6.14.

Do not assume from this information that the V7 chord in a key (or key-of-the-moment of major quality) necessarily takes the lydian ♭7 scale or the altered scale. The variety of approaches to playing on a dominant seventh chord is such that any possibility could be made to sound familiar or normal to us, depending upon context.

Example 6.15.

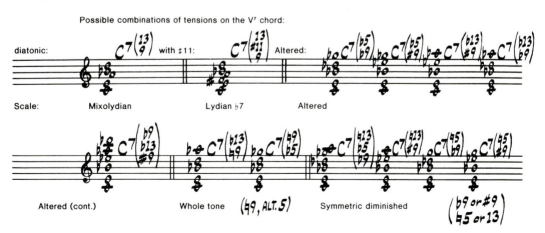

Examples 6.15 illustrates the use of the possible combinations of a altered and diatonic tensions on the V⁷ chord. Considerations of style and melodic context determine the appropriateness of one or the other of these choices.

Some theorists argue that substitute dominants in a key are more likely to take the lydian flat-seven scale and that it is the presence of the altered scale, or of altered tensions, in the melody on a dominant seventh that implies or generates dominant substitution. While this may be true in certain specific cases (see chapter 8), it seems that any type of tension is equally likely to occur on a dominant seventh or its substitute in the general sense. Also, only local melodic circumstances create a specific sense of the propriety of one type of tension or the other. For this reason, we simply note that a given dominant chord, whether it contains altered or natural tensions, has a functional substitute (with a root at the exact middle of that scale) that could share the same resolutions. We also note that those tensions altered in sound on the original dominant are natural in sound on the substitute, and vice versa (see example 6.16).

Example 6.16.

The two situations represented by these scales do not account for every possible combination of tensions on a dominant seventh chord, however. So far we have accounted for the possibility of both the ninth and fifth to be altered and for both of them to be natural tensions. What about scales, and their corresponding chords, in which the ninths are altered and the fifths natural, and vice versa? If we follow our pre-established rules regarding tensions, we can create these scales easily.

First, let us consider the case of the altered ninth and natural fifth. We combine the lower tetrachord of an altered scale and the upper half of a lydian flat seven scale on the same root. What results is a G7 which could adopt any of the following chord symbols: G7(♭9); G7(♯9); G7(♭9, 13); G7(♯9, 13). Any of these forms could also be implied by the chord symbol G7(♭9 or ♯9) when the natural fifth or thirteenth is established melodically.

Example 6.17.

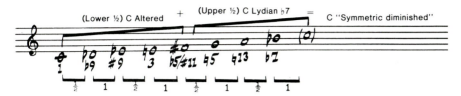

The scale we obtained is known as the *symmetric diminished* scale and is useful not only in these hybrid dominant seventh/tension situations, but also on four different diminished seventh chords (discussed in more detail later). The important characteristic of this scale is its *symmetric* structure, which is comprised chordally of superimposed diminished seventh chords and intervallically of component tritones, minor thirds, whole steps and half steps. It is symmetric in terms of each.

Example 6.18.

4 pairs of tritones

Without specifically considering diminished seventh chords, we can examine the various tritone intervals contained in this scale to see how many different dominant seventh chords are implied by it. Does every tritone contained in the scale imply a different pair of dominant seventh chords which can employ the scale? No. As it turns out, the original tritone, B and F, which generated this scale, belongs to our V7 chord (G7) and its substitute, Sub V7/I (Db7). Notice that, unlike the substitute dominant pairs discussed earlier, in this case both chords have the *same* formula: altered ninth, natural fifth.

Example 6.19.

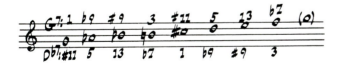

Examining the other tritones in the scale and the dominant seventh pairs they imply shows that not all would work with this scale.

Example 6.20.

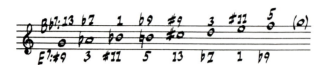

Example 6.21.

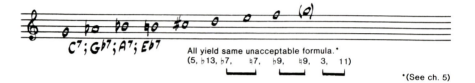

All yield same unacceptable formula.*
(5, ♭13, ♭7, ♮7, ♭9, ♮9, 3, 11)

*(See ch. 5)

In summary, we have found a scale useful for four different dominant chords within the key—V7/I and V7/VI and their substitutes Sub V/I and VI—all with the same types of tensions, altered ninth and natural fifth or thirteenth.

Example 6.22.

G⁷; B♭⁷; D♭⁷; E⁷ (All acceptable): 1, ♭9, ♯9, 3, ♯11, 5, 13, ♭7

Another way of stating this set of relationships is that the symmetric diminished scale yields the same intervallic formula and the same set of tensions from four equidistant points in the scale, any of which that could be the tonic. As a result, only three such discrete scales exist (see chapter 12).

In terms of our original problem we find that the substitute for V7 (altered ninth and unaltered fifth and thirteenth) is its tritone substitute, but with the *identical,* as opposed to the reciprocal, qualities for its extensions.

This same process of combining the upper half of an altered scale with the lower tetrachord of a lydian flat-seven scale yields the *whole-tone scale,* which is also symmetric, but from *every* pitch it contains rather than alternate pitches.

Example 6.23.

Lower ½ Lydian ♭7 + upper ½ Altered = "Whole tone" scale

Thus, we would possibly have an augmented seventh or dominant seventh (♭13 or ♯5) chord available based on every note in any given whole-tone scale. Just as with the diminished scale for any V + 7 or V7(♭13) chord, the related Sub V chord also has the parallel, as opposed to the reciprocal, types of tensions (altered fifth and thirteenth, natural or unaltered ninth). Table 6.2 summarizes the dominant seventh chord scale relationships.

Table 6.2. Dominant Seventh Chord Scale Relationships.

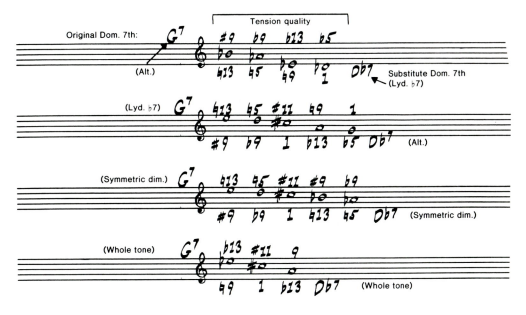

Finally, we observe that in almost all cases where dominant substitution is involved, the change in the root causes the change in the tension relationships, while the actual scale and chords involved stay the same.

Exercises

Exercise 6.1. Supply the following secondary dominants in the indicated keys:

Exercise 6.2. Supply the following substitute dominants in the indicated keys:

Exercise 6.3. Supply the substitute dominants *for* the following dominant seventh chords:

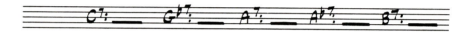

Exercise 6.4. Write out the indicated scales (see Table 6.1):

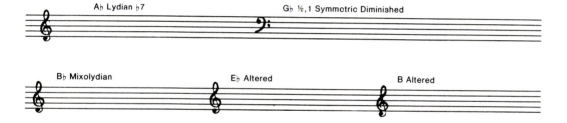

Exercise 6.5. Fill in the blanks:

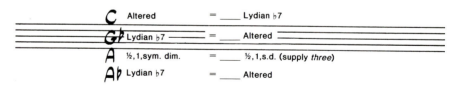

Exercise 6.6. List the four dominant seventh chords with an altered ninth and a natural fifth and thirteenth that employ the following scale (see example 6.22):

Exercise 6.7. List the six dominant seventh chords with an altered fifth and a natural ninth that employ the following scale:

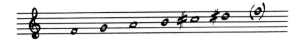

Exercise 6.8. Name the following scales:

Exercise 6.9. Place appropriate Roman numeral analysis above the following chord progression:

---

bibliography for further study

Coker, Jerry. **Improvising Jazz.** Englewood Cliffs, NJ: Prentice-Hall, 1964.

————. **The Jazz Idiom.** Englewood Cliffs, NJ: Prentice-Hall, 1975.

Delp, Ron. "Contemporary harmony: guide tones in improvisation." **Musician, Player & Listener** 19 (1979): 70.

————. "Contemporary harmony: progression—guide tones." **Musician, Player & Listener** 17 (1979): 72.

————. "Contemporary harmony: more on guide tones." **Musician, Player & Listener** 18 (1979): 72.

Haerle, Dan. **Jazz Improvisation for Keyboard Players.** Lebanon, IN: Studio P/R, 1978.

————. **Scales for Jazz Improvisation.** Lebanon, IN: Studio P/R, 1975.

LaBarbera, Pat. "Playing on changes." **Canadian Musician** 2 (1980): 67.

————. "Extensions & alterations on II-7, V7, Imaj7." **Canadian Musician** 2 (1980): 64.

Markewich, Reese. **Inside Outside: Substitute Harmony in Jazz and Pop Music.** New York: n.p., 1967.

McGhee, Andy. **Improvisation for Saxophone: the Scale/Mode Approach.** Boston: Berklee Music, 1974.

Patrick, James. "Charlie Parker and harmonic sources of bebop composition: thoughts on the repertory of new jazz in the 1940s." **Journal of Jazz Studies** 2 (1975): 61–85.

Pressing, Jeff. "Towards an understanding of scales in Jazz." **Jazzforschung/Jazz Research** 9 (1977): 25–35.

Strunk, Steven. "The harmony of early bop: a layered approach." **Journal of Jazz Studies** 6 (1979): 4–53.

Taylor, Billy. "Jazz improvisation: Bebop part 1," **Contemporary Keyboard** 6 (1980): 74.

————. "Jazz improvisation: chord substitution." **Contemporary Keyboard** 6 (1980): 56.

————. "Jazz improvisation: substitute patterns and devices for small left hand." **Contemporary Keyboard** 5 (1979): 86.

nonfunctional harmony

7

This chapter addresses the use of chords and cadences that normally have tonal function in nonfunctional ways. Most common are nonfunctional dominant chords.

A dominant seventh chord has functioned tonally if the following conditions occur:

   1. It is followed by a chord whose root is a perfect fifth lower.

Example 7.1.

   2. It is followed by a chord whose root is a half step lower.

Example 7.2.

   3. It is followed by a chord that is cadentially related to either of the above.

Example 7.3.

   4. It is followed by nothing at all.

Example 7.4.

Therefore, dominant sevenths not following one of the above-described patterns of resolution may be thought of as having no function harmonically. This engenders a fourth type of Roman numeral analysis for any given dominant seventh in addition to those of primary, secondary, or substitute dominant functions—the *nonfunctional* analysis. Taking F7 as an example, it might be the *primary* dominant seventh. In this case, the key or key-of-the-moment expected (although not necessarily the actual destination) is B♭:

Example 7.5.

(Expected)

It might be a *secondary* dominant, in which case (see chapter 4) the expected targets of resolution could be B♭-7 or B♭7 (as V7/II, III, IV, V, or VI).

Example 7.6.

It might be a *substitute* dominant seventh, which would have the same potential targets as those expected when it was a secondary or primary dominant. Now, presumably because of a change in key, the expected function is different.

Example 7.7.

Finally, it might be used in any of the following nonfunctional ways. These categories are developed according to their relative commonality of use.

First, it might be used as a tonic chord in the blues (see chapter 11). In this case, the chord most likely to follow has a root a perfect fifth or a half step lower (again, see chapter 11), but the harmonic rhythm and the fact that this chord is indisputably tonic (for example, a point of origin and return) are both legitimate criteria for the designation of this chord as "I7."

Example 7.8.

Second, it might operate as a IV7 in either a blues or following a traditional major or minor tonic chord.

Example 7.9.

As in "On a Clear Day"; "Jitterbug Waltz"

Since the most frequent occurrence of a dominant seventh chord on the fourth degree of the scale is in the context of the blues, we refer to such chords as IV7. As with other analytical descriptions of dominant chords, we want to account for the expected or predominant use of the chord, which in the case of the IV7 is not functional in ways discussed to this point. Just as F7 is V7 in the key of Bb because that is its statistically most prevalent function in that key, so it is IV7 in the key of C because of its use in the blues context. Again, remember that this particular designation does not preclude the possibility of functioning in other, unexpected (deceptive) ways.

Another blues-related and nonfunctional use of the dominant seventh occurs when the chord that is usually Sub V/V in the key simply is featured in a back-and-forth (vamp) type of progression between itself and the I chord. This chord is known as bVI7 in such instances and may work equally well in major or minor tonality. The bridge of "Georgia" and the A section of "Angel Eyes" exemplify each.

Example 7.10a.   *Example 7.10b.*

As in "Angel Eyes"   As in "Yardbird Suite"

Very frequently, as in example 7.10a above, this chord is found at a similar point in the phrase structure of the chord progression as IV7 might be.

Let us examine what happens with a substitution for IV7 (see chapter 6).

Example 7.11a.

First, in a simple tritone substitution we call the resulting chord VII7, as distinguished from V7/III, because it does not resolve but rather is used in a repetitive, vamp type of progression. Another means of arriving at VII7 is by combining the tonic diminished seventh (see chapter 11), Io7, with an appoggiatura leading-tone VII in the bass.

Example 7.11b.

The basic difference in sound between these two origins of the VII7 chord is in the chord scales associated with each. The former origin of the VII chord probably necessitates the use of a harmonic minor from the fifth scale (see chapter 4). The latter origin implies use of the ½, 1 symmetric diminished scale (see chapter 6).

Example 7.11bi.

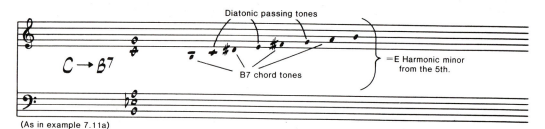

(As in example 7.11a)

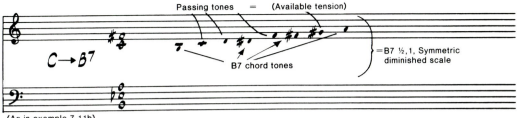

Passing tones = (Available tension)

B7 chord tones

= B7 ½,1, Symmetric diminished scale

$C \rightarrow B^7$

(As in example 7.11b)

Each of the following examples represents a different set of extensions used in the coloration of the VII7 chord. As a consequence, each implies a different origin for the chord.

Example 7.11c.

$F^7 (I^7)$ $E^7 (\overline{\text{VII}}^7)$ $F^7 (I^7)$ Uses Mixolydian; as in a Blues.

Example 7.11d.

$F^7 (I^7)$ $E^7 (\overline{\text{VII}}^7)$ $F^7 (I^7)$ Uses Altered; functioning as $\overline{V}^7/\overline{\text{III}}$

Example 7.11e.

$F^7 (I^7)$ $E^7 (\overline{\text{VII}}^7)$ $F^7 (I^7)$ Uses ½, 1 symmetric diminished. (See Ex. 7.11b)

As in "Groovin' High"

Example 7.11f.

$F^{\triangle 7} (I)$ $E^7 (\overline{\text{VII}}^7)$ $F (I^\triangle)$ Uses Lydian ♭7

As in "I Remember You"

The VII7 chord, then, contains many ambiguities, and generalities regarding specific chord scales and/or coloration seem not to apply to it (see table 7.1 later in this chapter).

Applying the same substitute relationships that yielded VII7 to the ♭VI7 chord creates the II7 chord, which is normally expected to function as V7/V.

Example 7.12a.

From "Chelsea Bridge"—See Appendix 3.

This chord occurs in inversions also, functioning much as a passing diminished chord might (see chapter 12).

Example 7.12b.

This usage might be a holdover from classical harmony brought to contemporary music via the Gospel tradition.

Finally, two other dominant chords frequently used in this manner are ♭III7, used often in a rhythm and blues context (example 7.13), and ♭VII7, which may be regarded also as a modal interchange chord (see chapter 8).

Example 7.13.

Example 7.14.

As in "Killer Joe" by Benny Golson

Since many dominant chords might be either functional or nonfunctional, it is important to analyze them according to their actual use. Do not use the system of nomenclature in this chapter except to account for the specialized and relatively rare uses of the harmonies outlined here. The entire concept of harmonic analysis would be meaningless if Roman numerals were assigned arbitrarily to chords merely on the basis of their distance from the tonal center. The following examples illustrate this point:

Example 7.15.

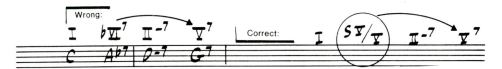

Example 7.16.

Nonfunctional dominant sevenths, even though their related II-7's may precede them (see example 7.11e), generally do not resolve, and they return to I in lieu of resolution.

A topic related to nonfunctional dominant sevenths is nonfunctional cadences, in particular II-V's. Since the same criteria that determine the function of a cadence determine the dominant seventh chord contained within it, the first category of nonfunctional cadences is those in which the dominant seventh is nonfunctional.

Example 7.17.

As in "Groovin' High"

The second, and most common, of these nonfunctional cadences is the chromatically ascending II-V. These have two basic uses. First, they can be used to approach the legitimate II-V in the key.

Example 7.18.

As in "Moment's Notice" by John Coltrane

Second, they are useful in creating modulation (see chapter 9). In this case the familiarity of the sound of the cadence is exploited as it is repeated. It thereby helps to shape the form of the composition or individual phrase within it.

Example 7.19.

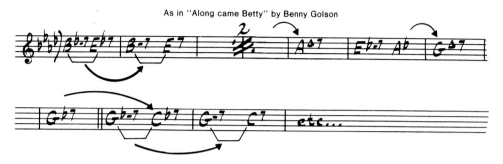
As in "Along came Betty" by Benny Golson

One final effect in nonfunctional harmony is the use of a particular chord structure that repeats without regard to its function, simply for the sake of organizing the piece according to the repetition and recognition of the familiar sound. Any chord or cadence might cause this effect. As with the nonfunctional dominants discussed above, it is often possible to postulate functional analysis for some of the chords involved in such a progression. Yet a more discerning aural examination of such progressions yields the conclusion that such descriptions are inappropriate. Some examples follow:

Example 7.20a.

II - 7's   In minor thirds

Example 7.20b.

Dominant sevenths ↑ m3ʳᵈ; ↓ +4ᵗʰ   ...etc...

Example 7.20c.

Δ7's   In minor thirds   ...etc...

See "Forest Flower" by Charles Lloyd;
    "Tell Me a Bedtime Story" by Herbie Hancock

exercises

Exercise 7.1. Analyze the following chord progression using Roman numerals:

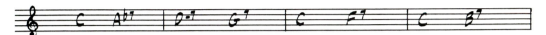

Exercise 7.2. Analyze the following chord progression using Roman numerals. Compare it to exercise 7.1:

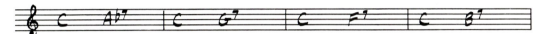

Exercise 7.3. Analyze the following chord progression:

discography for further study

"Along Came Betty." **Art Blakey and the Jazz Messengers, Moanin'**. Blue Note 84003.

"Blue Monk." **Monk's Greatest Hits.** Columbia CS 9775.

"Forest Flower." **Charles Lloyd At Monterey.** Atlantic 1473.

"Groovin' High." **Charlie Parker and Dizzy Gillespie, Echoes of An Era.** 2-Roulette RE-105H.

"I Remember You." **Charlie Parker: The Verve Years.** Verve Records VRVE Ve2-2523.

"Jitterbug Waltz." **Everest Records Archive of Folk and Jazz Music: Eric Dolphy.** Everest Records EVR FS227.

"Killer Joe." **Quincy Jones, Walking In Space.** A&M SP 3023.

"Ladybird." **Smithsonian Collection of Classic Jazz.** Columbia P6 11891.

"Moment's Notice." **Blue Trane.** Blue Note 81577.

"Nostalgia in Times Square." **Nostalgia in Times Square,** Charles Mingus. Columbia Records #35717.

"On A Clear Day." **On A Clear Day You Can See Forever.** RCA LSOD-2006.

"Tell Me A Bedtime Story." **Fat Albert Rotunda.** Warner Brothers S-1834.

"There Is No Greater Love." **Miles Davis: Four & More.** Columbia Records SPC #9253.

minor key harmony and modal interchange

8

We have mentioned previously that various forms of minor are interchangeable. Within any composition in a minor key, we often find chords that are diatonic to all three forms of minor and/or the minor modes. Yet each form of minor makes an important contribution to the overall context of minor tonality. To understand this, let us begin by deriving the diatonic harmony for each.

The simplest place to start is with the *aeolian* mode, also known as *natural* or *pure minor*. Since natural minor is also one of the diatonic modes in the major scale (the one associated with VI-7; see chapter 2), we have already derived its diatonic harmony when we did so for its related major scale, known as the *relative* major. Thus, we simply describe the original diatonic chords in the relative major in relation to the new tonic, which was the sixth degree of the original major scale.

Example 8.1.

Next, we displace the tonic of the series of Roman numerals, making the A-7 the I chord. Applying the Roman numerals, we now describe the identical series of harmonies with the tonic A as follows:

Example 8.2.

We follow this same process to yield the diatonic harmonies for all of the remaining modes of the major scale. Therefore, we establish the diatonic harmony for the aeolian mode.

Next, we examine the distinctions between the newly-derived aeolian harmonies and those of the related major scale. To compare them, we use the roman numeral system to see them as *parallel* systems.

Example 8.3.

The important distinctions are that the minor system has tonic-related chords, known as tonic minor, I-7 and ♭IIIMaj, containing the lowered third distinctive to the key, and also that this minor system contains *no dominant seventh* on the fifth degree, but rather a minor seventh. The traditional V-I cadence used in major key chord progressions is not available in aeolian minor. The strong tritone resolution we associate with the V7-I cadence in major is not present and extraharmonic means, such as repetition and long duration of the I chord, establish the fact that the I-7 is the tonic chord. This is extremely difficult to do, and this explains why modal chord progressions that are not in major tonality tend to be more repetitive and simple. They also contain more extended durations within tonic areas than do tonal progressions. The question is whether the modal cadence V-7 to I-7 is strong enough to be effective harmonically or whether alteration is necessary to this harmonic system to make it more effective cadentially and capable of competing with major key harmony. The original II-7-V7 cadence from the relative major is still present, but now it is called IV-7-♭VII7. Oddly enough, this particular cadence exists rarely in actual minor key music. Perhaps this is true because it so strongly suggests a resolution down a fifth to a major chord, which would establish the relative major tonality, inadvertently converting the progression IV-7-♭VII7-I-7 back into the familiar II-7-V7-I in the related major key a minor third higher. The Roman numerals reflect the way we actually *hear* a progression. Especially where borrowing of chords from minor tonality for use in parallel major tonality *(modal interchange)* occurs, we must be sure that the effect of the chord progression is accurately reflected in the tonal center that our Roman numerals imply. For example, we could analyze the following progression in the aeolian mode. However, its harmonic rhythm and the placement of the cadence is such that this analysis would not reflect the musical reality of the situation—that what we have is a standard major key chord progression.

Example 8.4.

A serious weakness of the aeolian mode as a tonal system is that its lack of distinctive harmonies or cadences tends to sublimate it in importance to its relative major. This is by far the most common use of the harmonies generated by the aeolian mode: as sources of modal interchange chords which appear frequently in the *parallel major* to enrich the diatonic system. (*Parallel* major/minor scales have the *same* root and different harmony, for example, *C major* versus *C minor. Relative* major/minor scales contain the *same pitches* but do not share the same tonic, for example, *C major* and *a minor*.) The most useful among these are the following: IV-7-♭VII7, ♭VIMaj, ♭IIIMaj, and II-7(♭5), (which most often occurs in the context of a cadence and is therefore more correctly thought of as derived from harmonic minor.) The other diatonic chords in aeolian, I-7 and V-7, nearly always occur as related II chords of cadences leading to secondary key areas (see chapter 4) and are not really generated in relation to the aeolian mode. This brings up the next step, which is the further expansion of the diatonic system to include both the important potential uses for the modal interchange chords and related cadences that might precede them. Especially common among these are II-V's of modal interchange chords, such as ♭VI Major 7 and ♭III Major 7. It is also possible to have deceptive resolutions of secondary dominants in a key (to modal interchange chords), as well as extended or substitute dominant progressions which could approach II or V chords or modal interchange chords. "Ladybird," by Tadd Dameron (see discography), is a good example of a composition that establishes a series of secondary key areas using modal interchange chords in conjunction with traditional secondary key areas from parallel major tonality.

Example 8.5.

We can make some simple tritone substitutions of dominant seventh chords in the same chord progression in order to illustrate the potential for deceptive resolution of secondary dominants, as in example 8.6.

Example 8.6.

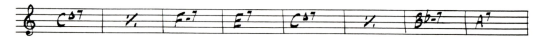

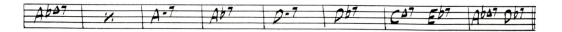

How do the predominant melody notes sound in relation to the new dominant seventh chords? What is the proper analysis for these chords? Notice the predominance of E naturals on the B♭7 chords. Since this cadence (IV- to ♭VII⁷) is used so frequently in the parallel major as a modal interchange progression, we almost expect B♭7 to move up a step cadentially to the I chord. To underscore this activity, the ♯11 is evident in the melody of improvisation on this particular chord. It implies the use of the chord in major tonality, being the major third of the key superimposed upon the ♭VII7 chord.

A general guideline that provides an acceptable option for a minor key chord scale, especially with an entire cadence extracted, is to improvise or write over the given chord(s) using the scale that generated the chord, treating the root of the chord as the momentary center of gravity for the scale. Common exceptions to this rule are the use of the *locrian* mode on -7(♭5) chords and the *dorian* mode on II-7 chords wherever they are used cadentially. A tune of harmonic characteristics similar to "Ladybird" is "What's New" (see discography), which actually vascillates between major and minor tonality.

Example 8.7.

Even with the expanded harmonic possibilities made possible by introducing the modal interchange concept, chords occur in the previous two examples that elude our analytical skills. And despite the tonal inadequacies inherent in the aeolian mode, music in minor tonality exists. We can solve both of these problems by examining the diatonic harmony generated by the remaining forms of minor and the other minor modes.

To begin, let us alter the aeolian mode to give us a V7 chord instead of a V-7 by raising the seventh scale degree (leading tone) and thereby restoring it to its natural state.

Example 8.8.

By doing this, we affect all the diatonic harmonies in the aeolian mode in one way or another, either by changing the quality of the seventh chord (since the leading tone is one of the chord tones) or by changing the nature of the available extensions (because the leading tone is one of the passing tones/extensions in the scale.)

Example 8.9.

Diatonic harmony from Harmonic Minor + available tensions

Again, we see the crucial nature of the types of passing tones used in improvisation or composition. There is a clear difference in the implications of a V7-I cadence in contrast to those of a V7(♭9, ♭13)-I cadence. In restoring the leading tone of the key to the scale, we retain the minor quality of the tonality (the I chord is still minor) yet establish a dominant seventh chord on the fifth degree. The resulting scale is *harmonic* minor. In the interaction of the three forms of minor in the same composition we can re-examine "What's New" as an example of combining model interchange harmony from aeolian with the cadence from harmonic minor. This all then leads deceptively to a tonic chord from the parallel major. The harmonic analysis of that progression in example 8.10 shows the source of each chord and describes its use.

Example 8.10.

When a chord is diatonic to one or more modes or scales on the same root (for example, A♭ major seven might be diatonic to harmonic or natural minor), which mode should be used for choosing the extensions of the chord? Again (refer to chapter 4), the choice is that of the player. As long as the player remembers to consult the melody to avoid potential clashes, the scalic source chosen may be (1) the one that yields the largest set of potential tensions (most richness) or (2) the one that most accurately reflects the context or direction of the chord progression. It depends upon whether horizontal or vertical considerations are most important at a particular point in a composition or improvisation: momentary richness (greatest number of available tensions) or tonal direction (inclusion of certain passing notes to imply a particular scalic source, key area, or eventual destination). One very common alteration to the expected scale that is an example of the former process is the transformation of the V7(♭9, ♭13) scale from harmonic minor, starting on the fifth scale degree to the altered scale (see examples 8.12 and 8.13).

Example 8.11.

Example 8.12.

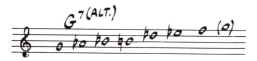

The reason for this alteration is that, aside from the root and the tritone, the only important points of potential harmonic stability in the chord would be ♭9 and ♭13, and each implies another note in an altered pair of tensions. This replacement is common in secondary dominants of II, III, and VI also. However, one might derive an actual voicing (V7 [♯9, ♭5], for example) from such a scale that no longer directly implies the chord's function as the dominant of a minor chord. The reason this substitution works is that altered dominants (see chapter 11) frequently resolve to major or other dominant target chords and, aside from V7(♭9, ♭13) in particular, create no specific expectation of resolution. To illustrate this, play the two following cadences in example 8.13.

Example 8.13.

Did either one sound any more deceptive or normal than the other? Although V7(♭9, ♭13) may be a possible expression of the altered scale, its particular diatonic derivation might also be from harmonic minor. Conversely, although it is acceptable to *interpolate* the altered scale over V7 of a minor chord as a result of the harmonic implications of the tensions ♭9 and ♭13, an altered dominant does not necessarily imply a resolution to a chord of minor quality.

To this point we have discovered the use of natural minor in generating modal interchange chords and of harmonic minor in creating the potential for an actual V7-I cadence in a minor key. But what of melodic minor and the remaining modes of minor quality? What contributions can they make to music in minor tonality or to modal interchange situations?

Melodic minor goes one step further in the adjustment of the minor mode that occurred in the transition from aeolian to harmonic minor. Melodic or "jazz" minor retains the leading tone and restores the lowered sixth to its original natural quality. Then we have arrived at a scale that resembles a major scale with a minor third. (Note that melodic minor in jazz theory is different from melodic minor as seen in traditional harmony; there is no provision made for the descending form, which is really simply the aeolian mode.) That is why this particular scale is so pivotal in linking blues and minor tonality—it is actually a major scale with a blue note replacing the third (see page 128). You can assume a similar process when discussing the addition of the flatted seventh scale degree to create the dorian mode.

Example 8.14.

The reverse set of consequences has occurred in example 8.14 in contrast to the changes in chord tones and tensions that resulted when moving from aeolian to harmonic minor. The most important changes presented here are in the quality of the I chord and in the relationship between the melodic minor scale and dominant seventh scales discussed in chapter 6. However, there is also a new type of minor seven flat-five chord, VI-7(♭5), which contains a *natural* nine.

Example 8.15.

C-Δ7   D-7   Eb+Δ7   F7   G7   AØ7   BØ7   B7(ALT.)

Diatonic harmony from Melodic Minor + available tensions

A minor seven (b5) chord always occurs a half step above a major seven chord, and vice versa, a relationship that yields a common reharmonization.

Example 8.15a.

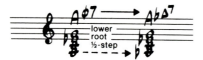

In major key voice-leading, the major seventh chord often is followed by the major sixth chord in the final two bars of a four-bar cadential harmonic phrase to create the illusion of smoothly continuing harmonic rhythm and sequence.

Example 8.16.

The same effect can be achieved in minor if melodic minor is an available source for the tonic chord.

Example 8.17.

Since most players freely interchange major seven and six on major and minor chords, melodic minor becomes an important scale for generating tonic or temporary tonic minor harmony. It is also important for another reason: a melodic minor scale is really the scalic source for the altered dominant and lydian flat-seven scales. For example, C-6(9) = F7($\sharp$11) = B7(alt), all because they are each related to the same scale.

Example 8.18.

The B7 is not diatonic in the strict sense to melodic minor, but enharmonics reign in contemporary harmony, and the interrelationship between these chords and their correspondent scales cannot be ignored simply because it does not exist technically. As we will see later, this relationship becomes particularly interesting in the context of blues-related reharmonization.

Finally, let us expand our diatonic system just a bit further by including in it a few commonly used chords from the remaining unexamined diatonic modes. First of all, we consider the minor modes. Example 8.19 lists the diatonic chords and extensions for the parallel dorian, phrygian, and locrian modes (see table 8.2 also).

Example 8.19.

Example 8.19—Continued

C Phrygian

C Locrian

Most commonly used and distinctive among these options are ♭IIMaj7 and ♭VII-7 (from phrygian), the cadence I-7-IV7 (from dorian, and also minor blues-related), and ♭VIIMaj7 (also from dorian). In "Ladybird" (see example 8.5) are examples of ♭VII-7 (although it is used as a related II-7 in a cadence as opposed to a modal interchange chord) and especially of ♭IIMaj7, used commonly in the context of the modal interchange cadence or *turnaround* I-♭IIIMaj7-♭VIMaj7-♭IIMaj7-I. (This could also be reharmonized with the same root pattern but using dominant sevenths on alternate chords. This use would provide alternating deceptive and normal resolutions of substitute dominants in the key, a favorite interpolation at the turnaround often used by John Coltrane: I-SV/II-♭VI-SV/I.)

Finally, we consider the remaining major modes, lydian and mixolydian (again, refer also to table 8.2).

Example 8.20.

C Lydian

C Mixolydian

Mixolydian contributes the unique I7, which loses much of its potential for truly modal sound due to the influence of blues (although this is a possibility; see "All Blues" by Miles Davis). This influence has conditioned us to hear a I7 initially as a blues chord rather than a mixolydian modal chord. Notice also that the dominant seventh, wherever it occurs in modal harmony, has the relatively bland set of tensions, natural nine and thirteen, associated with the mixolydian mode of the major scale. Mixolydian also contributes the III-7(♭5), often functioning as the related II of the secondary dominant V7/II. It can be thought of as the source of ♭VII major 7, in which the diatonic chord VII$^{\emptyset7}$ has had its root replaced by a blue note (see example 8.15a). The context dictates whether this is heard as a dorian chord, a mixolydian chord, or simply a diatonic VII-7(♭5). The lydian mode contributes a II7 again, with natural tensions and no ♯11, V Major7, VII-7, and ♯IV$\emptyset$7, a commonly used chord in a variety of tonal contexts. These contexts could be a deceptive resolution of V7, a related II of V7/III, a passing between IV and V or vice versa, a substitution for II7, or a related II of IV7 in a chromatic cadence.

Example 8.21.

Common Modal Interchange Chords

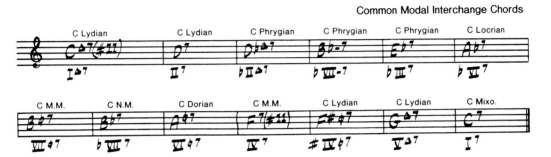

When there are so many potential scalic sources for any given type of a chord, some generalizations are helpful. They might not account for every possible use of a given type of chord but will greatly facilitate answers to the overall problem of what to do when confronted with a particular chord for the first time. The generalizations in table 8.1 are musically valid if the melody is judiciously consulted before they are used. All designations refer to the given mode based on the chord's own root.

Table 8.1.

Chord Type	Scale (Based on Chord's Root)
Minor 7th	Dorian
$\emptyset$7ths	Locrian
$\Delta^{7's}$; $\Delta^{6's}$	Lydian (except IΔ^7)
o7ths	1 step, half step, symmetric diminished
+7ths	Whole tone
Nondiatonic dominant 7ths	Lydian ♭VII^7
Secondary dominant 7ths	*Altered* if preceding resolution to an expected *minor* chord.
	Lydian ♭7 or *mixolydian* if preceding resolution to an expected *major* or dominant chord.

Since these are generalizations, there are many exceptions to them, both in terms of the actual function of the chords involved and in potential melodic clashes because of certain tensions. However, familiarity with all of these scales and the different chord types with which they are associated on all twelve possible roots is a good start when looking for the raw materials needed for potential sources of harmonic stability within the context of an improvisation or composed melody.

The information in this chapter could be summarized by updating the skeletal diagram of the expanded diatonic system as follows in table 8.2.

Table 8.2.

Chord Type

Basic diatonic system:		I△	II-⁷	III-⁷	IV△⁷	V⁷	VI-⁷	VII∅⁷
Secondary dominants:		—	V⁷/II	V⁷/III	V⁷/IV	V⁷/V	V⁷/VI	—
Substitute dominants:		SV/I	SV/II	—	SV/IV	SV/V	—	—

Extended dominants/or extended substitute dominants: Any dominant 7th chord found half step or P5th above any other dominant 7th or its related II-⁷ or II∅⁷

Extended II-V's: Any II-V or II-sub V cadence resolving down half step to *either* another -⁷ or dominant 7th in a similar cadence

Miscellaneous: II-V's moving up in half steps (to functional II-V's in the key)

Modal Interchange Possibilities:

Modes

Mode							
Natural minor	I-⁷	II∅⁷	bIII△⁷	IV-⁷	V-⁷	bVI△⁷	bVII⁷
Harmonic minor	I-△⁷	''	bIII+△⁷	''	V⁷($^{b13}_{b9}$)	''	VIIo⁷
Melodic minor	I-⁶	II-⁷	''	IV⁷	V+⁷	VI∅⁷	VII∅⁷ or VII⁷
Dorian	I-⁷	''	bIII△⁷	''	V-⁷	''	bVII△⁷
Phrygian	''	bII△	bIII⁷	IV-⁷	V∅⁷	bVI△	bVII-⁷
Locrian	''	''	bIII-⁷	''	bV△⁷	bVI⁷	''
Mixolydian	I⁷	II-⁷	III∅⁷	IV△⁷	V-⁷	VI-⁷	bVII△⁷
Lydian	I△⁷ (#11)	II⁷	III-⁷	#IV∅⁷	V△⁷	VI-⁷	VII-⁷

Finally, we need to distinguish between modal and tonal music. Elements of both may coexist in the same piece in the form of a modal section of a composition alternating with tonal ones. However, the general characteristics of a modal piece, or section of a piece, are the following:

1. Repetitious chord progression that is strictly diatonic to the mode and that could not in any way (root motion, use of tritone, etc.) be confused with a tonal chord progression implying a different key center than the one desired, especially the related major key

Example 8.22.

2. Special emphasis on the note or combination of notes that characterizes a particular mode uniquely

Example 8.23.

3. Avoidance of any nondiatonic melody notes other than very carefully used passing notes, and any cadence used in tonal contexts (including modal interchange cadences)

Example 8.24.

Strictly modal music often sounds simple, but it is difficult to write and play because of its many restrictions. Much more common is the combination of modal and tonal elements in the same composition. This achieves the desired space and variety characteristic of modal music without depriving the soloist or composer of the necessary harmonic structure of a strong progression.

Example 8.25.

(C Dorian) (C Phrygian) (C N.M.)

---

exercises

Exercise 8.1. Name the relative minors of the following keys:

Exercise 8.2. Name the parallel minors of the following keys:

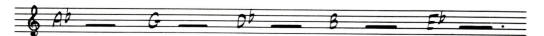

Exercise 8.3. Write out the diatonic harmony in the following keys; then in the space provided write out the diatonic harmony in each of their respective relative or parallel minor forms as indicated:

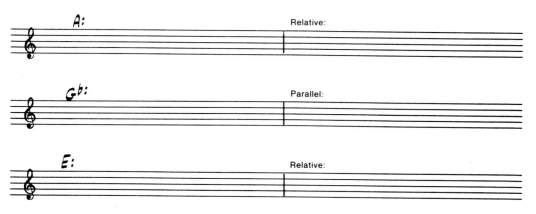

Exercise 8.4. Analyze the following chord progression using Roman numerals (see examples 8.6 and 8.7):

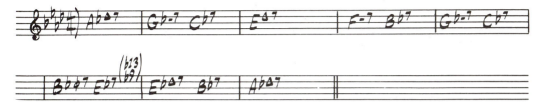

Exercise 8.5. Write out the diatonic harmony, including available tensions, in the following melodic or harmonic minor keys as indicated (see examples 8.8 and 8.15):

Exercise 8.6. Supply the appropriate chord scales for the chords contained in the following progression (see table 8.1):

Exercise 8.7. Circle the modal interchange chords in the following example:

Exercise 8.8. Write out the altered and harmonic minor from the fifth scales for the following dominant seventh chords, labelling them after the fashion of the first example (see examples 8.11 and 8.12):

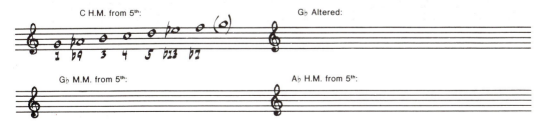

Exercise 8.9. Give three different names for each of the following scales (see example 8.18):

(Roots)

Exercise 8.10. Label the modes from which each of the following chord progressions were generated; then analyze the given progressions using Roman numerals:

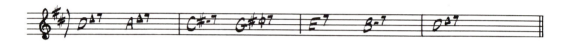

Exercise 8.11. Analyze the following chord progression using Roman numerals and give the parallel mode from which each modal interchange chord was borrowed (see example 8.21):

Exercise 8.12. Write eight-bar modal progressions and melodies in the following modes (see examples 8.23 and 8.24):

C Lydian

Gb Phrygian

bibliography for further study

Berle, Arnie. "Fretboard basics: primary chords of modes." **Guitar Player** 13 (1979): 146, 166.

de Rose, Nino. "Il jazz modale." **Musica Jazz** 36 (1980): 2–6.

Goyone, Daniel. "L'improvisation modale." **Jazz Hot** 376 (1980): 42–43.

Kühne, Willem. "De modale blues van Rein: muziek profiel." **Jazz / Press** 49 (1978): 20–22.

Welburn, Ron. "Some limits to modal improvising today: the Sonny Rollins example." **The Grackle** 5 (1979): 22–24.

discography for further study

"Moment's Notice." **Blue Trane.** Blue Note 81577.

"What's New." Ballads, John Coltrane. Impulse A32 / AS32.

"Ladybird." **Smithsonian Collection of Classical Jazz.** Columbia P6 11891.

9 modulation

Modulation is the process of changing keys. There are three different ways of moving from one key to another: (1) by using chord(s) common to both keys, (2) by using chords common to neither key, or (3) by passing through a series of temporary, or only briefly established, keys which finally settle permanently in the new key. In most modulations, form plays an important role. A modulation at the completion of a phrase is much more commonplace or predictable to our ears, for example, than a modulation within a phrase, which is consequently much harder to effect.

The first method of modulation is the *pivot modulation*. The following chord progression is a simple pivot modulation in which the common cadence II–7–V7 in the old key is heard simultaneously as a borrowed modal interchange cadence in the new key. Notice that in analyzing the progression Roman numerals for both keys indicate that the chords in question are being heard concurrently in both keys.

Example 9.1.

Pivot modulations using other harmonic devices we have studied also exist. One example is the use of extended substitute or chromatic dominants and II–V's.

Example 9.2.

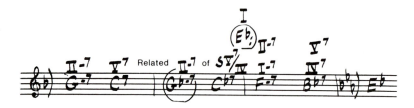

Modal interchange chords from the modes are also useful, as in "All the Things You Are"

Example 9.3.

The important point is that in a pivot modulation no time passes without a sense of key and that, at least briefly, the chord progression is heard in both the old and new keys.

The second and also very common form of modulation is *direct modulation.* In direct modulation, we establish a new key in one of two ways. We may establish it abruptly by beginning a new phrase in a new key at a strategic location such as the bridge of the tune. Or, the new key is established when at a certain point the chord progression can no longer be analyzed logically in the old key. This means that technically nonexistent Roman numerals (which do not appear in Table 8.2) would be applied. Direct modulations of this latter type occur less often, and when they occur within the logic of a particular harmonic progression, it is often due to the phenomenon known as *constant structure* (see below).

"All the Things You Are" (see example 9.3) has examples of direct modulation, one occurring where the bridge or consequent melody of the tune is expected (because of its regularity of phrase length or because of its strategic location in the *form.*)

Example 9.4.

The other direct modulation follows as a harmonic and melodic sequence in the development of this new idea, but indisputably in its own new key.

Example 9.5.

On the other hand, direct modulations that result from deceptive resolutions of standard harmonic progressions exploit a predictable sequence of chords known as *constant structure*. The modulation in example 9.6 works as a result of a standard modal interchange turnaround extended to include all the key-related major seventh chords. However, it then establishes its own momentum as a result of the harmonic sequence thereby created and subsequently moves into the new key nearly unnoticed.

Example 9.6.

The interesting thing about this chord progression is that it could just as easily have remained in the original key (see chapter 8) and have been heard that way.

Example 9.7.

Finally, direct modulations within a melodic phrase are possible if the strength and logic of that phrase are strong enough to prevent the modulation from sounding awkward. Such modulations were a favorite of John Coltrane. The first phrase of ''Giant Steps'' (see appendix 1) is a good example.

Example 9.8.

The third, rarest, and most abstract type of modulation is the *transitional modulation*. During a transitional modulation, a series of chords, often in some kind of internally logical pattern, move through a series of temporary keys which are dealt with so briefly as to not really be established tonally. In addition, the end result is the arrival in a key different than the one preceding the transitional period. Just as with modal harmony, melodic phrasing and development must be extremely good to assure musicality in the absence of traditional dependence on harmonic organization in establishing or defining the form. This first excerpt, ''Chelsea Bridge''

(see appendix 3), moves from the key of E through the temporary area of G major (strongly related via modal interchange to the tonality of E) and finally uses extended dominant and substitute dominant root motion to arrive at the key of Db, the original key of the piece.

Example 9.9.

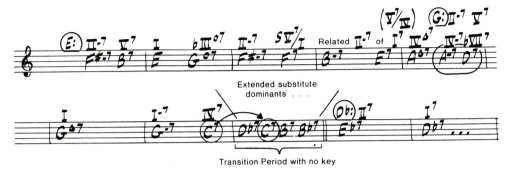

Extended substitute dominants . . .

Transition Period with no key

Turning a chord of major or dominant quality into a minor seventh on the same root (which then is involved in a cadence) is a common building block in the formation of all types of modulation (see chapter 5). Examples of this are found in "Ornithology," "How High the Moon," and the bridge of "Joyspring" by Clifford Brown.

Example 9.10 relies entirely on melodic development and repetition for its formal organization, since whatever key has been established at the beginning has clearly been transposed by the ninth bar. Benny Golson uses a series of deceptive resolutions and ambiguously brief harmonic episodes to arrive at the new key (see chapter 7). Determining the key in the beginning is difficult since the presence of cadences a half step apart leaves the first key unresolved.

Example 9.10.

From *"Along Came Betty"* by Benny Golson

Same as measures 1&2

Modulation is a tool composers or arrangers use to create more interest in a piece. Normally, a modulation helps define the form of a piece. Therefore, formal barriers should be our first stop in searching out modulations. However, placement of modulations in unexpected areas, particularly when they do not coincide with melodic phrasing, can be a device that has the potential to lend interest, momentum, and cohesiveness to a composition. When we discuss reharmonization in chapter 12, we consider interpolation of transitional modulations where direct ones previously existed, primarily at the formal seams of a piece.

The key to understanding modulation is knowing what functions every chord or type of chord in tonal use could have.

exercises

Note: For the purposes of the exercises in chapters 9 through 13 ⌢ = dom7 resolving down by a perfect fifth to any chord; ⌊⌋ = a II-7 V7 cadence; ⌒↘ = dom7 chord followed by any chord a half step lower; and ⌊---⌋ = a min7 chord followed by a dom7 a half step lower.

Exercise 9.1 Analyze the following modulations and identify their type (pivot, direct, or transitional):

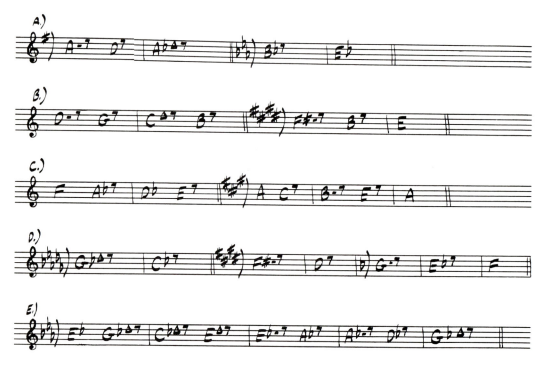

Exercise 9.2. Fill in the chords in the following modulations according to the Roman numeral analysis provided; then identify them by type as in exercise 9.1:

---

bibliography for further study

Legido, Alvaro. "Les harmonies du jazz." **Jazz Magazine** 263 (1978): 22–25.
————. "Les harmonies du jazz, part 2." **Jazz Magazine** 264 (1978): 36–38.
————. "Les harmonies du jazz, part 3." **Jazz Magazine** 265 (1978): 41–43.

---

discography for further study

"All The Things You Are." **Sidney Bechet / Martial Solal: When A Soprano Meets a Piano.** Inner City Records IC 70008.
"Along Came Betty." **Art Blakey and the Jazz Messengers, Moanin'.** Blue Note 84003.
"Chelsea Bridge." **Ellington Songbook.** Verve VE–Z–2535.
"Giant Steps." **Giant Steps.** Atlantic SD 1311.
"Joyspring." **Daahoud.** Mainstream MRL 386.
"Ornithology." **Charlie Parker on Dial, Vol. 1.** Spotlight 101.

10 rhythm

In the previous chapter we discussed the mechanics and methods involved in harmonic and melodic embellishment. Now let us discuss the most important element in the development of one's musical ideas in jazz—*rhythm.* It is important to develop an understanding of how to use rhythm in order to play or write successfully in the idiom, but too intellectual an approach to the subject stifles the spontaneity expected in jazz. Consider this topic, more than any other, as a series of generalizations to apply to specific musical situations as taste and experience dictate, *not* as a collection of rules. It is up to the student to study rhythmic practices in the various styles of jazz and draw conclusions concerning the validity of these generalizations. Remember this essential disclaimer as we examine some stereotypical rhythmic concepts associated with the jazz idiom.

Jazz Eighths

Perhaps no single musical effect contributes more to our feeling that the music we hear is jazz than the player's interpretation of eighth notes. When Duke Ellington wrote, "It don't mean a thing if it ain't got that swing," he was talking about the listener's perception of the basic *feel* of the music. Discussions of the authenticity of musical feeling in jazz inevitably revert to the interpretation of the eighth note. Because jazz has historically been primarily a player's music, the written interpretation of the swing eighth note has caused many theorists and composers considerable consternation. For example, the identical melodic passage played by two different players might swing to varying degrees, or not at all. Therefore, no *written* example explains the difference in interpretation between music that does and does not swing. Listen to the difference, however, between the interpretation of melodic lines of eighth notes in the right hands of pianists such as Bud Powell, Lennie Tristano, or Herbie Hancock (see examples in discography for this chapter). Then listen to your favorite recording of any Mozart or Beethoven piano sonata containing eighth notes in scalar passages. The difference in feel is quickly apparent.

In most jazz settings the composer or arranger can achieve a comparable effect by indicating "swing eighths" on the part in lieu of, or in addition to, other sytlistic markings. A great many composers seeking to introduce this sort of musical feel to players unschooled in the jazz tradition use the notation:

Example 10.1.

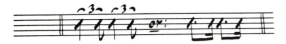

However, it is this author's opinion that the indication of a triplet notation introduces yet other stylistic connotations (see later in this chapter). The experiments of those seeking to precisely notate the swing eighth note are invariably less successful than their interpretation by players familiar with the idiom. One can easily see that such notation is unnecessarily complex in contrast to simple eighth note presentation.

Example 10.2.

Syncopation

While not uniquely indigenous to jazz styles, syncopation of rhythms is common and works frequently in combination with swing eighth notes to produce melodic fragments with a jazz feel. Syncopation involves the displacement of on-the-beat notes to a position in the measure which is off the beat; in other words a portion of the melodic phrase is shifted to a position in the measure that usually is one-half a pulse earlier or later. It therefore accents a different part of the phrase.

Example 10.3.

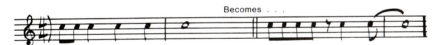

The following three examples illustrate typical rhythmic syncopations in jazz and demonstrate how they might evolve from simpler, on-the-beat rhythmic patterns. The actual number of attacks remains the same as the syncopation occurs. Analyze each example to see exactly where and how each syncopation takes place.

Example 10.4a.

Example 10.4b.

Example 10.4c.

Notice the difference in sound and feel between syncopated and unsyncopated rhythms. The composer/arranger must distinguish between the two or risk inadvertently writing a straight rhythm where a swinging one was intended. When syncopation involves a melody note that is also associated with a change in harmony, the accompanists in the rhythm section adjust the harmonic rhythm accordingly. For an accomplished rhythm section this would not need to be notated (see Example 10.5a), but for an uninitiated one it might be necessary (see Example 10.5b).

Example 10.5a.

Example 10.5b.

Notice the symbols used in writing parts for the accompanying instruments. Basically, the composer/arranger is giving these instructions to the instrumentalist:

    1. Play a specific chord in the given rhythm. Do this by using stemming notation as one would in normal rhythmic notation, with the difference being

that enlarged, diamond-shaped notes or diagonal slashes substitute for normal noteheads. These should be large enough so that they are not confused with specific pitches.

Example 10.6a.

2. Play the chord in the indicated rhythm using a specific attack or *accent.* Accents apply for instrumentalists of any kind according to the following prescribed uses. Note that these may differ from those used in traditional instrumental practice.
   a. The *short* attack leaves space between the given attack and the next one. It is most common in cases involving consecutive off-the-beat attacks (as in example 4a above) since this type of articulation is awkward to execute at relatively fast tempos if the eighth note immediately following the attack is articulated.

Example 10.6b.

   b. The *accented* attack should not directly precede another articulated eighth note without at least an eighth note's worth of space intervening. It can occur in many of the same situations as the short attack but frequently involves a syncopation at the point of chord change (see examples 10.5a and 10.5b above): *

Example 10.6c.

   c. A note may be held its *full value, without any accent* in articulation. This articulation might immediately precede either of the above instances or simply be used as a desired legato effect regardless of a surrounding syncopated context.

Example 10.6d.

(Notice phrase-markings)

These accents and articulations evolved from common usage and in many cases are redundant for more experienced players. At times, however, a specific phrasing or interpretation requires their use, even for experienced players. Young players can also employ them as a learning tool to gain a sense of phrasing and idiomatic interpretation.

Rhythmic Variations and Their Effects on Style

Since rhythm is such an important factor in jazz music, it is logical that it contributes to the distinct styles of jazz. The most important distinction exists between styles that are purely swing-derivative and styles in which harmonic and melodic elements blend with the rhythmic elements of other styles of music, most notably Latin styles and rock styles. In swing styles the eighth notes are played in a swing style, while in most Latin or rock-influenced styles they are not. Often the same figure presented in the context of a different type of pulse is interpreted in two different ways. A good hint as to the correct interpretation of these figures is that when you find yourself snapping your fingers on ''2'' and ''4'' (with the drummer's hi-hat cymbal), you have swing eighth notes.

Example 10.7a.

Example 10.7b shows one possible execution of the typical swing beat on the drum set. Notice that cymbals, since they are of indefinite pitch, are notated with the Xs while the drums utilize actual noteheads.

Example 10.7b.

If the feel of the music is in *two,* or cut-time the same rhythmic figure might be interpreted as straight or even eighth notes. These distinctions in styles are easy to spot; with music in two, the sixteenth note is the basic subdivision of the pulse, and in the earlier swing examples, the eighth note is the smallest subdivision. To illustrate this point, let us see how the identical rhythmic figure might be presented in swing and in two. Note that the effects of the cut meter and halved metronome marking cancel one another out. Although the figure looks more complex, it probably sounds identical with the first, save the difference in interpretation. The composer/arranger who is aware of this distinction can decide upon the meter to be used according to the desired stylistic effects.

Example 10.7c.

While a comprehensive discussion of Caribbean and South American styles of jazz would entail many more pages (see chapter 10 bibliography), we can generalize concerning three or four important rhythmic styles. In some of these styles the major distinctions involve changes in accompaniment patterns more than in melody or harmony. Most Latin beats played by jazz drummers are really transcriptions of instrumental parts played by Latin American and Caribbean folk and dance ensembles, adapted to the traditional drum set. (Compare example 10.10 (below) with the following transcription of a typical mambo beat in example 10.7d. It is interesting to see which adaptations are made as the jazz drummer strives to imitate the Latin percussion section.)

Example 10.7d.

Jazz musicians frequently use the *bossa nova* beat. This medium-tempo Latin beat uses straight eighth notes and syncopations. In addition to its tempo (it is always felt in 4/4), it can be identified by the presence of some of the following rhythmic patterns in the accompanying instruments (drums, piano, guitar), as seen in example 10.8.

Example 10.8.

The *samba* is basically a double-time bossa nova. In addition to the pulse on the downbeats, which it shares with the bossa nova, it typically incorporates a busier and more active harmonic and melodic rhythm. The drummer usually plays more on the drums than on the cymbals. The overall effect of the samba is of more active, agitated music, with the drumming achieving at times a nearly military flavor.

Example 10.9.

Good examples of bossa nova in jazz can be heard in the Stan Getz/Astrid Gilberto collaborations, most popular among them being ''The Girl From Ipanema.'' The composer A. C. Jobim also recorded many albums that contain classic representations of the bossa nova in jazz. For the jazz samba, Chick Corea's ''You're Everything'' (see chapter 10 discography) is a good example. The coexistence of jazz and Latin styles in the same composition is also common. A good example of an integration of the bossa nova and swing beats in the same composition is "Forest Flower" by Charles Lloyd (see discography).

Occasionally described as Afro-Cuban or Afro-Latin, the *jazz mambo* is borrowed from the mambo. Its use in jazz can be traced clearly to the inclusion of Cuban percussionists in Dizzy Gillespie's ensembles of the late '40s and early '50s. The most celebrated examples of it would be in such compositions as "Night in Tunisia" and "Cubana Be." It was not long before drummers and composers incorporated this adapted mambo into their work. In 1953, Max Roach interpreted this beat (in example 10.10) in playing Teddy Edwards' "Sunset Eyes" (transcription; compare with Example 10.7d).

Example 10.10.

Later in the decade, it became common to integrate the jazz mambo and swing beats in the same composition, alternating between the two for contrast. Horace Silver was well known for this, and two particularly noteworthy compositions of his involving this practice are "Yeah" and "Nica's Dream" (see discography). This beat may be employed at varying tempos.

A modern cousin to the various Latin styles is *salsa,* a dance style employing sophisticated jazz harmonies and orchestrations and featuring an emphasis on brass and percussion. In the practice of the rhythm section it differs from the samba mostly in the presumption of a larger percussion section. This results in a slightly different role for the bass player, whose part normally features many syncopated attacks, particularly quarter-note anticipations.

Example 10.11.

This brief discussion can only introduce the variety of effects of Latin American music upon jazz. Further study can provide more stylistic nuances in composing and arranging, especially for the rhythm section.

One additional type of music that occasionally involves the use of straight eighth notes is jazz tempered by the influence of rock music. This is basically an outgrowth of the interaction of rhythm and blues and jazz during the 1960s. Such music features the use of the simpler, more repetitious harmony of the rock idiom. It also reinforces the style of rock through the use of straight eighth notes and a sixteenth note subdivision of an on-the-beat pulse. The extended improvised solos of this style gave rise to the term "jazz-rock." Examples of this accessible style of jazz range from popular recordings by such groups as Blood, Sweat and Tears to Freddie Hubbard (for example, "Red Clay") and Herbie Hancock (for example, "Wiggle Waggle"; see discography).

Other Uses of Rhythm

Although the placement and subdivision of the basic pulse of the music has a good deal to do with differentiating swing-oriented jazz from other styles, rhythm may affect style without changing the basic pulse of the music. These effects usually involve changes in *harmonic* and *melodic rhythm,* which constitute the rate of frequency or density of melodic and harmonic activity. Be-bop, for example, usually involves a rapidly paced and relatively predictable harmonic and melodic rhythm. While rhythmic displacement is often present in the classic postwar jazz style, be-bop generally involves a fast, steady stream of eighth notes over a chord progression moving at an equally steady rate. Reconsider "Donna Lee" by Charlie Parker, as seen in example 10.12.

Example 10.12.

Syncopation and embellishment are very important factors in conveying the rhythmic feeling of be-bop.

In the late '50s and early '60s, however, the *modal* style evolved (see chapter 14). Part of this new style of jazz was a greater rhythmic feedom. In order for it to contrast with the previously established be-bop style, the new modal music initially conveyed a feeling of less predictable and persistent harmonic and melodic rhythm. Gradually, the use of simple ostinato patterns as a vehicle for soloing in the modal style became popular; thus a repetitive harmonic foundation provided the opportunity for rhythmic freedom during solos. John Coltrane's interpretation of "My Favorite Things" is a cornerstone of this style, while "Orbits" and "Delores" by Wayne Shorter show the use of rhythmic unpredictability in constructing modal melodies (see discography). In any case, the jazz of the '60s increasingly emphasized rhythm over harmony.

The use of *polyrhythms,* or the coexistence of more than one subdivision of the bar operating at the same time, takes many forms in jazz, some commonplace, some quite esoteric. A very common polyrhythm in both melody and accompaniment is the 12/8 feel, associated with an older style of blues.

Example 10.13.

Variations on this triplet subdivision of the 4/4 quarter note include 9/8 and 6/8, although the latter may also be a result of the concurrent playing of 3/4 and 4/4 patterns (see example 10.15).

Example 10.14.

Example 10.15.

Such polyrhythms may also occur melodically or during solos. They form the basis of many drum solos, as they display the drummer's coordination.

Finally, the emphasis placed upon polyrhythms and rhythm in general in the late '50s and early '60s led to experimentation of jazz composers with *polymeters,* such as 5/4, 7/4, and 7/8. A polymeter is made up of some combination of duple and triple meters and care must be taken in writing melodic and harmonic rhythms in such meters so that the intended subdivision of the bar is clearly indicated.

Example 10.16.

Good examples of jazz in compound meter are "Take Five" by Dave Brubeck, "Man From South Africa" by Max Roach, and any of the compositions from the album *Electric Bath* by Don Ellis (see discography).

For an interesting study of music exploring more fully the potential of percussion instruments and rhythm, listen to "M Boom," a recent all-percussison album by a group led by Max Roach.

exercises

Exercise 10.1. Rewrite the following melodies in the space provided, showing the use of syncopations and appropriate articulations:

Exercise 10.2. Write out bass lines for the following melodic fragments in the indicated styles:

bibliography for further study

Aikin, Jim, trans. "Lennie Tristano's introduction to 'Intuition'." **Contemporary Keyboard** 6 (1980): 61.

Barr, Walter. "The Salsa rhythm section." **NAJE Educator** 12 (1970/1980): 15–18, 48–50.

Bartz, Jerzy. "Pursuing the essence of swing." **Jazz Forum International Edition** 47 (1977): 61–63.

Brown, Theodore Dennis. "A History and Analysis of Jazz Drumming to 1942." 2 vols. Ph.D. dissertation, University of Michigan, 1976.

Di Cioccio, J. "Prime source: pure modern jazz drumming." **Woodwind World, Brass and Percussion** 16 (1977): 40.

Encyclopedia of Rhythms. New York: Da Capo, 1976.

Forman, Steve. "South American percussion: Cuica speaks." **Down Beat** 18 (1979): 80–81.

Giuffre, Jimmy. **Jazz Phrasing and Interpretation.** New York: Associated Music Publishers, 1969.

Goldberg, Norbert, "South of the border: Brazilian percussion." **Modern Drummer** 3 (1979): 46–47, 57.

———. "South of the border: the Mambo." **Modern Drummer** 3 (1979): 36–37.

———. "South of the border: New directions in Latin drumming." **Modern Drummer** 4 (1980): 42–43.

Inocencio, Rivera. **The Bass Player's Guide for Modern Latin Rhythms.** Boston: Reno Music, 1969.

Kofsky, Frank. "Elvin Jones part 1: rhythmic innovator." **Journal of Jazz Studies** 4 (1976): 3–24.

———. "Elvin Jones part 2: rhythmic displacement in the art of Elvin Jones." **Journal of Jazz Studies** 4 (1977): 11–32.

LaPorta, John. **Developing Sight-reading Skills in the Jazz Idiom.** Boston: Berklee Press, 1967.

———. **A Guide to Jazz Phrasing and Improvisation.** 2 vols. Boston: Berklee Press, 1972.

Magadini, Peter. **Musician's Guide to Polyrhythms.** 2 vols. Hollywood: Try Publishing, 1970.

Mehegan, John. "Tonal and rhythmic principles." **Jazz Improvisation.** Vol. 1. New York: Watson-Guptill, 1959.

————. "Jazz rhythm and the improvised line." **Jazz Improvisation.** Vol. 2. New York: Watson-Guptill, 1962.

Miles, Butch. "Learning the chart and phrasing." **Modern Drummer** 3 (1979): 38–39.

Mintz, Billy. **Different Drummers.** New York: Amsco Music, 1975.

Roberts, John Storm. "Latin persuasions: a brief overview of a vital musical genre." **Down Beat** 44 (1977): 13–14, 52.

————. **The Latin Tinge: The Impact of Latin American Music on the United States.** New York: Oxford University Press, 1979.

Rogers, Milt. **The Bossa Nova Method.** New York: Criterion, 1952.

Smith, Arnold Jay. "Mongo Santamaria: Cuban king of congas." **Down Beat** 44 (1977): 19–20, 48.

Taylor, Billy. "Jazz improvisation: the clave." **Contemporary Keyboard** 5 (1979): 63.

Thigpen, Ed. **Rhythm Analysis and Basic Co-ordination.** Copenhagen: priv., 1977.

Wolfe, George. "Rhythmic innovation in the jazz combo." **NAJE Educator** 11 (1979): 56–60.

discography for further study

The Amazing Bud Powell. 2 vols. Blue Note BLP 1503–1504.

"The Blues." **Folkways Jazz, Vol. 9.** Folkways FJ 2809.

"Crosscurrent." **Smithsonian Collection of Classic Jazz.** Columbia P6 11891.

"Cubana Be." **Manteca,** Dizzy Gillespie. Camden Records QJ–25211.

"Delores," **Miles Smiles.** Columbia PC 9401.

Descent Into the Maelstrom. Inner City 6002.

"Donna Lee." **Charlie Parker: Bird is Free.** Apex Records PLP–401.

"Electric Bath." **Electric Bath,** Don Ellis. Columbia Records CS–9585.

Electric Bath. Columbia CS–9585.

"Man From South Africa." **Percussion Bitter Sweet.** Impulse 8.

M'Boom. Columbia IC–36247.

"My Favorite Things." **My Favorite Things.** Atlantic 1361.

"Nica's Dream." **Horacescope,** Horace Silver. Blue Note BLP–4042/84042.

"Orbits." **Miles Smiles.** Columbia PC 9401.

"Sunset Eyes." **The Best of Max Roach and Clifford Brown in Concert.** GNP Records GNP #S18.

"Take Five." **Time Out.** Columbia PC 8192.

"Wiggle Waggle." **Treasure Chest.** Warner Brothers 2WS 2807.

"Yeah." **Horacescope,** Horace Silver. Blue Note BLP–4042/84042.

"You're Everything." **Light As A Feather,** Chick Corea. Polydor PD 5525.

blues

11

In our discussion of theory so far we have neglected the a priori of all contemporary music—*blues*. The reason is that, in addition to having generated a series of derivative musical forms in American music (of which jazz is one), the blues make an excellent testing ground for learning how to employ these new theoretical tools. Blues avoids most technical pitfalls encountered in applying the principles of jazz improvisation elsewhere. It is difficult to get lost in a blues, since the landmarks are so obvious and the form so logical. Most importantly, when playing a blues progression, a student with a good ear and sense of phrasing can make any note sound right in any harmonic situation. What is there is the nature of blues form, harmony, and melody that makes all of this possible?

Let us review the nature of the blues form, although this is an overgeneralization of a lengthy historic process. Basically, blues is a form derived from the concept of antecedent (or dependent) and consequent (or independent) melodic ideas—"call" and "response." (The complementary and recognizable imitation between the two related ideas is a more important formal device than the harmonic base of these initial melodic statements, most typically the I^7 and IV^7 chords.) Generally, this imitation occurs in the first two bars, with the third measure resembling the first and melodically leading to a point of rest in the fourth bar. This point of rest defines the end of the first phrase and invites the improvisor to take melodic and harmonic liberties in order to direct us to the fifth bar of the form. This is the bar in which the material from the first two bars is either repeated on the level of the IV chord or repeated untransposed despite the presence of the IV harmony. The succeeding complement to this repetition is the same melodic material used in measures three and four, usually on the I chord, which again leads to a point of melodic inactivity in the eighth bar. This lets the soloist direct us toward the next important part of the structure, which would be a cadence in the ninth and tenth bars, usually accompanied by a new and independent melodic idea. Next, in the eleventh and twelfth bars two bars of tonic sound or tonic elaboration follow harmonically, perhaps in the form of some improvised turnaround. Structurally speaking, the most important elements in identifying the basic twelve-bar blues forms are summarized in example 11.1.

Example 11.1.

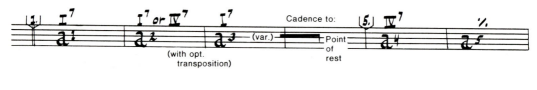

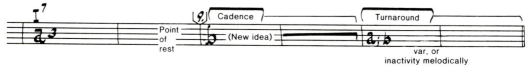

It is not necessary for all of these elements to be present in a piece of music for it to represent a blues form. Our ears are more concerned with the motivic structure of the blues than with a strict adherence to the most standard harmonic form (see examples that follow). Another important point is the vocal influence of the evolution of the blues form. Accommodations have been made in the form for breathing, giving a clear definition to each phrase. The melody in example 11.2 illustrates the formal structure outlined above.

Example 11.2.

BLUE MONK—Monk

A long history of compositions similar to that just examined establishes an aural tradition. An intuition on the part of its listeners and players enables the innovative writer to exploit one aspect of the form at the expense of another, thereby giving the structure a new, yet recognizable, twist.

Example 11.3.

Nostalgia in Times Square—Mingus

The above composition clearly depends for its effect on the standard notion of the motivic nature of blues structure. The composer has changed the standard harmonic structure present in the previous compositions in order to focus attention on the varying uses of the Eb7 chord on which the harmonic progression now depends (instead of the expected Bb7). Whether or not the given piece is still harmonically a blues is irrelevant. What is important is that it could not exist without the expectations created by the blues form. In the absence of the blues form it would have no point of comparison or stylistic meaning.

Blues is more than a twelve-bar harmonic form. Certain idiomatic melodic inflections are characteristic of blues as well. To illustrate this, compare a transcription of a West African baliphone ensemble (Example 11.4) with a well-known melody from the Western European tradition of composition. This second melody was written before the American interaction (of the Western European style of composition) with the West African melodic-contrapuntal tradition.

Example 11.4.

Example 11.5.

Piano Sonata K.545—Mozart

Since instrumental music mainly follows and imitates the vocal music of a culture, these two examples represent a well-preserved distinction of the two musical cultures that collided in southern America near the turn of the nineteenth century. The most evident point of comparison is the more angular and rhythmic nature of the first. (For an interesting discussion, compare the melody shown in example 11.4 with the dominant seventh chord scales explained in chapter 6, or with the "French sixth chord," if you have a background in traditional music theory.)

Another important distinction is the presence of the cadence, and in fact the conscious use of harmony, both literally and in the form of arpeggiation and scales in the European example. This is in opposition to a mere presence of a tonal center in the West African one where harmony evolves merely as a function of the coincidence of improvised melodies and their contrapuntal interaction.

Finally, there is the rhythmic element. The African example is more sophisticated and rhythmically involved. Almost any improvisatory insturmental folk music found outside of the European tradition places a more significant emphasis on the use of rhythm as a structural element than does European classical music.

Although these are only two representative examples of musical traditions, each much more involved and diverse than could be indicated in a few pages, these distinctions and emphases apply in a general way. One of the points at which these two melodic traditions meshed in America was in the Black Southern church, where the vocal traditions of Western Africa were tempered to the demands of chorale-style voice-leading, exemplified in the chord progressions of church hymns. In this interaction the most common melodic intervals to be added to the European diatonic scales and harmonies occurred a minor third, augmented fourth, and minor seventh above the tonic of the key. The practice of leaping to a nonharmonic tone, then treating it as an appoggiatura to another note in the scale was employed with any pitch, whether or not the pitch itself was in the scale. Thus, any note in the chromatic scale eventually could be given the effect of a *blue note,* depending upon whether it had the potential for being a melodic auxilliary to a chord tone at a given point in the harmonic progression. In example 11.6, the simple I-IV-V-I progression so common in chorale-style harmony has the blue notes 1, ♭3, and ♭7 in the key placed above the chords.

Example 11.6.

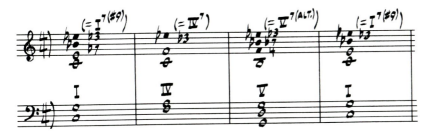

This process had the effect of creating an entirely different set of acceptable blues harmonies as a variety of blue notes became treated as acceptable extensions of chords rather than as mere appoggiatura. The standard blues progression can feature I7, IV7, and V7 in virtually any form—major or minor, altered or unaltered—and in any combination. Many of the most common chords in jazz evolved as a result of placing blue notes above the traditional key-related harmonies discussed in earlier chapters. The following short examples illustrate the ways in which different notes within the chromatic scale can have the properties of either blue notes or targets of blue note resolutions depending upon changing harmonic situations.

Example 11.7.

Later in the development of jazz, as the basis for improvisational structure evolved to include more harmonically sophisticated forms of popular music, its players and composers found blues providing an inexhaustible variety of new relationships between itself and the new harmonies. Often, blues melodies from one key were used with harmonies from an entirely different key, thereby implying a new, *pantonal* (in more than one key) approach to playing and improvising. For example, "Daahoud" by Clifford Brown (see appendix 3a) has a melody whose tonal center is indisputably E♭ throughout, although, since it is a blues-related melody we are unable to tell from the melody itself whether it is E♭ minor or major. The lowered third in blues has a potentially ambiguous function either as a chord tone or blue note.

Example 11.8.

Daahoud—C. Brown

Yet the chord progression that accompanies this melody exemplifies transitional modulation, implying two keys with only the second one sharing the same tonal center as the melody. We explore this interrelationship fully in chapter 13, which discusses pentatonic scales and harmony built in fourths.

Example 11.9.

Clearly blues melody provides the basis for an improvisational conception that is inherently developmental because of the nature of blues phrase structure. A player or writer attuned to the intuitive demands of melodic development inherent in blues melody brings that same sense of coherence to improvisation or writing regardless of the harmonic situation. We have seen how composers use blues-related melody in a variety of tonal situations to manipulate our expectations for melodic resolution and to create new relationships between melody and harmony. Blues melody notes add an idiomatically necessary coloration to the predictable scenario of smooth, scalewise diatonic melody.

The basic twelve-bar blues harmonic form can incorporate all the technical devices discussed in earlier chapters. Most of these variations occur by interpolating differing cadential patterns to approach the strategic points of the progression, namely the fifth and ninth bars. These coincide with the phrase breaks inherent in the vocal blues tradition (see example 11.2). For example, the fourth bar frequently contains a cadence to the IV7 chord, and the presence of blue notes from the key in the melody allows for either I7(alt) or SV7/IV to accomplish this harmonically (see Ch. V).

Example 11.10.

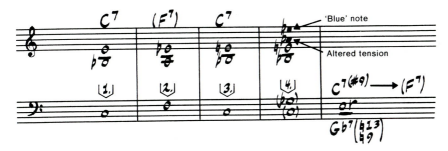

In many blues Charlie Parker extended this process backwards to produce the type of progression in example 11.11 (see also Ch. V).

Example 11.11.

Example 11.12.

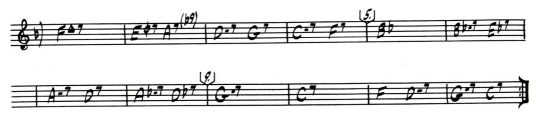

The basic blues form can be truncated following the move to the IV chord. This is common practice in compositions that feature one eight-bar section of a blues-related tune, such as the A section of "Confirmation" by Charlie Parker (see also chapter 12).

Example 11.13.

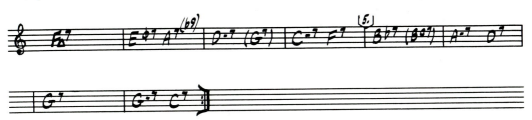

Other variations possible for reharmonizing within a blues solo, on the part of a rhythm section as well as the soloist, include use of substitute chords for the important structural chords, such as a VII7 (see chapter 7) replacing the traditional IV7.

Example 11.14.

Finally, not every blues structure needs twelve bars. The most common variations involve extension of normal phrase lengths and displacement of the location of the IV and V chords, as for example in "The Work Song."

Example 11.15.

*Typical minor blues cadence

Blues in 3/4 or 6/8 are often twenty-four bars in length since their phrasing incorporates a harmonic rhythm that changes only half as frequently as the number of measures involved, for example in "Footprints" by Wayne Shorter.

Example 11.16.

In conclusion, we see blues affecting every element of our musical heritage. Many melodies not used directly in blues owe their motivic structure to the call and response nature of blues that conditions our sense of melodic development. Hearing the repetition of the same motif over different chord changes is also part of our conditioning as blues listeners. The use of blue notes or blues phrases within the context of tonal chord progressions as an adjunct to strict diatonic playing is indispensable to idiomatic jazz playing or writing. And, finally, the traditional blues harmonic form can be altered or enhanced to produce sections of larger song forms, or blues forms of unorthodox length.

Let us examine the following hypothetical improvisation/embellishment of the original example of European melody (example 11.5) with which we began the chapter. Notice the use of tonal devices (discussed in earlier chapters) in this example. Also note the use of blue notes as passing notes and their effect on the coloration of certain harmonies.

Example 11.17.

---

exercises

Exercise 11.1. Complete a twelve-bar blues in the AAB motivic format by developing the following motif as indicated (See example 11.1.):

Exercise 11.1—Continued

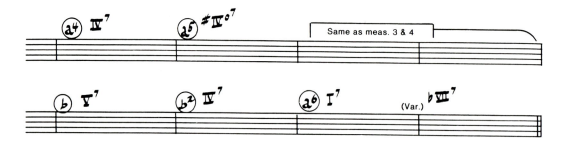

Exercise 11.2. Using the same melody as in exercise 11.1, write and analyze different chord changes from those in exercise 11.1 where indicated. Make chromatic alterations where the new chord symbols require it.

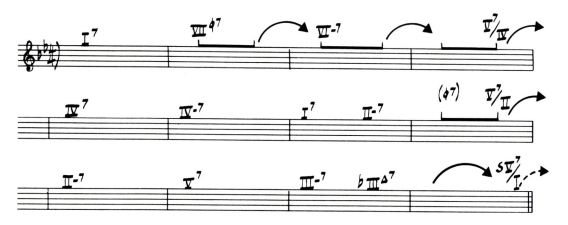

Exercise 11.3. Analyze the melody and harmony in the following example. Pay particular attention to motivic development and melodic analysis of blue notes:

"Ascent of Man"—Jaffe

bibliography for further study

Aiken, Jim. "The blues scale." **Contemporary Keyboard** 8 (1982): 28–29.

Beier, Ulli. "The talking drums of the Yoruba." **Journal of the African Music Society** 1 (1954): 24–31.

Blacking, John. "Some notes on the theory of African rhythm advanced by Erich von Hornbostel." **Journal of the African Music Society** 1 (1955): 12–20.

Brancel, Rose. **The Music of Central Africa.** The Hague: Martinus Nijhoff, 1961.

Cone, James. **The Spirituals and the Blues: An Interpretation.** New York: Seabury Press, 1972.

Coryell, Larry. "Contemporary guitar: major and minor blues progressions." **Guitar Player** 14 (1980): 112, 126.

DeLerma, Dominique-Réné. **Reflections on Afro-American Music.** Kent, OH: Kent State University Press, 1973.

Feather, Leonard. "African roots." **Melody Maker** 53 (1978): 6.

Handy, William Christopher, ed. **Blues: An Anthology.** New York: A.&C. Boni, 1926.

Jones, Arthur Morris. **Studies in African Music.** 2 vols. New York: Oxford University Press, 1959.

Keil, Charles. **Urban Blues.** Chicago: University of Chicago Press, 1969.

Mason, Bernard Sterling. **Drums, Tomtoms and Rattles: Primitive Percussion Instruments for Modern Use.** New York: Dover, 1974.

Nketia, J. Kwabena. **Drumming in Akan Communities of Ghana.** Edinburgh: Thomas Nelson & Sons, 1963.

————. **The Music of Africa.** New York: W.W. Norton, 1974.

Sackheim, Eric. **The Blues Line: A Collection of Blues Lyrics.** New York: Grossman, 1969.

Schuller, Gunther. **Early Jazz: Its Roots and Musical Development.** New York: Oxford University Press, 1968.

Shockett, Bernard I. "A Stylistic Study of the Blues as Recorded by Jazz Instrumentalists, 1917–1931." Ph.D. dissertation, New York University, 1964.

Simonini, Pierluigi. "La musica del'Africa Occidentale." **Musica Jazz** 33 (1977): 8–11, 13–14.

————. "Sopravvivenze africane nella musica Jazz." **Musica Jazz** 33 (1977): 8–11.

Smallwood, Richard. "Gospel and blues improvisation." **Music Educators Journal** 66 (1980): 100–104.

Spencer, Ray. "Piano talk no. 23: the twelve bar blues." **Jazz Journal International** 33 (1980): 13–14, 23.

Taylor, Billy. "Jazz improvisation: blues piano." **Contemporary Keyboard** 5 (1979): 72.

Varley, Douglas. **African Native Music, an Annotated Bibliography.** London: Dawson's of Pall Mall, 1970.

Williams, Raymond. **The African Drum.** Highland Park, MI: Highland Park College Press, 1973.

discography for further study

"Blue Monk." **Monk's Greatest Hits.** Columbia CS 9775.

"Blues For Alice." **Swedish Schnapps.** Verve 68010.

"Confirmation." **Return Engagement.** MGM V3HB–8840.

"Daahoud." **Daahoud.** Mainstream MRL 386.

"Footprints." **Miles Smiles.** Columbia PC 9401.

"Nostalgia in Times Square." **The Immortal 1959 Sessions.** Columbia 35717.

"Work Song." **The Japanese Concerts,** Cannonball Adderley. Milestone Records M–47029.

reharmonization

12

Reharmonization is the process of altering a given section of a chord progression by changing one or more of the chords in it. This change in progression usually intends to (1) improve the richness of the harmony and enhance its role in the presentation of a melody, and (2) increase the interest created in the chord progression itself as a vehicle for the improvisor / soloist. Reharmonization may have a primary interest that is either *vertical* or *horizontal,* depending upon whether or not it is intended as a device to be used primarily in supporting the melody or the improvised solo. According to this basic distinction, a variety of reharmonization techniques can be identified.

First, reharmonization may be accomplished in simple diatonic situations by replacing a given diatonic chord with another chord that functions the same way within the key, for example, tonic, subdominant, dominant. Observe the following alteration to the basic progression I-VI-II-V, for example.

Example 12.1.

In addition to changing the richness of the melody in relation to the harmony, such an alteration affects the overall shape of the melodic phrase as it is dictated by the movement within it toward the richest point. This often coincides with the cadence.

Another means of reharmonizing a section of a chord progression is to replace a chord with another one that shares common tones with it and that is not necessarily a chord with the same function. It may not even be diatonic. This is known as *third-related* reharmonization, since chords that share a given melody note as a common chord tone or tension often have roots a major or minor third apart.

Example 12.2.

In addition to simply replacing one chord with another related chord, it is possible to add chords in ways that reinforce the overall direction of a pre-existent chord progression.

Example 12.3.

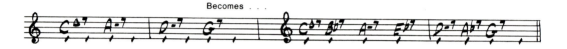

Notice the improvement in the above chord progression when the new chords are added. While no actual change in the progression has really occurred, the illusion of greater harmonic activity has been created, strengthening the overall interest in the phrase. Example 12.4 is a reharmonization that creates a more extended harmonic structure at a point where the progression had been inactive and relatively bland.

Example 12.4.

This emphasizes one of the most important principles of reharmonization: the most appropriate place to insert intense harmonic activity is a point of relative melodic inactivity. Let us examine some reharmonizations derived from standard melodic cliches that occur frequently in inactive points in chord progressions. First, there are those standard descending melodic lines used on stationary minor chords, sometimes known as *fallings sevenths.*

Example 12.5.

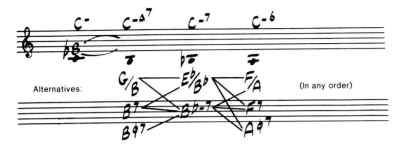

Alternatives: (In any order)

These same sorts of lines might ascend from the fifth.

Example 12.6.

Alternatives:

Finally, they might be made motivic if the chord progression contained other inactive minor chords, such as in a minor blues or blues-related composition.

Example 12.7.

Once lines like these have been extracted, they might constitute an alternative bass line or inner voice line. For example, look at the possibilities for the previous cliché in example 12.8.

Example 12.8.

Another similar line is often employed during the turnaround that occurs at the end of a typical blues, or rhythm changes, progression.

Example 12.9.

Among the more common of the possible reharmonizations for these two blues cliches are seen in example 12.10.

Example 12.10.

A good example of reharmonization at work is within the context of the repeating A section of the *rhythm changes* chord progression. Rhythm changes is the chord progression to the Gershwin tune "I've Got Rhythm," which has become the basis for hundreds of jazz and popular tunes since its establishment as a standard tune during the 30s and 40s. Examples in the jazz idiom include "Oleo" by Sonny Rollins and "Serpent's Tooth" by Miles Davis. Popular culture has even been influenced by this landmark progression; a good example is the theme from the television show "The Flintstones." Perhaps the reason for the popularity of this progression is that it contains so many harmonic clichés. The melody is a variant of the standard blues motivic structure, truncated to conform to the eight-bar phrase length of the AABA song form. Like a blues, it is composed melodically of two simple ideas and their variations.

Example 12.11.

The harmony to this melody is based on an elaboration of the I area with a series of common turnarounds (*see chapter 5*), or on two-bar progressions that fill up an otherwise harmonically inactive part of a chord progression and return to the I chord. This is then combined with a move to the IV-chord in the fifth bar—also like a blues.

Example 12.12.

Turnarounds, especially in blues music, are perceived more in terms of their root motion than in terms of the actual qualities of the chords involved. Therefore, a frequent means of reharmonizing such a segment of a chord progression is to change the qualities of the chords in the turnarounds so that they are all dominant, at the same time perhaps including some substitute dominant root motion where the phrase repeats.

Example 12.13.

Another common type of reharmonization within the context of this particular turn-around-based progression is the use of passing diminished sevenths (see chapter 5) or diminished seventh chords whose roots are found between two diatonically adjacent chords. In the case of the rhythm changes progression, ascending passing diminished seventh chords occur frequently. This is true because in enharmonic terms, any ascending diminished seventh chord is equivalent to the secondary dominant seventh ($\flat$9) chord, which would resolve to their common diatonic target chord, as illustrated in example 12.14.

Example 12.14.

Within the context of the rhythm changes progression, these might be used as follows in example 12.15:

Example 12.15.

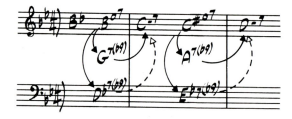

This leads to an important point concerning diminished seventh chord symbols. If a diminished seventh chord is followed by a chord whose root (or lowest note, if an inversion) is *farther* than a half step away, it is most likely a misnamed dominant seventh (♭9) chord (see example 12.16).

Example 12.16.

The exceptions to this rule are diminished sevenths which resolve to a chord with the same root. These are called *tonic* or *auxilliary* diminished seventh chords.

Example 12.17.

A specific exception to this rule is the instance of ♯IVo7 in the sixth bar of a blues-related progression when followed by a I chord in the seventh:

Example 12.18.

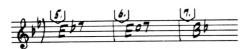

You can employ the symmetric diminished scale derived in chapter 6 on any ascending diminished seventh chord that is reharmonized with its related dominant seventh (♭9), whether V or SubV of the mutual diatonic target chord is used as the substitute.

Example 12.19.

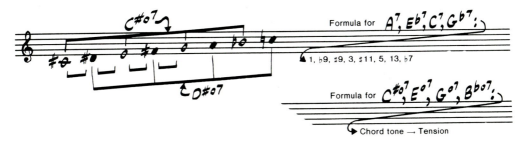

Next, we might alter the turnaround immediately preceding the last two bars of this progression by using diatonically-related chords derived from the obvious blues cliche counterline 1, ♭7, 6, ♭6, 5.

Example 12.20.

The chord progression to Thelonious Monk's composition "Humph" illustrates the process of backing up from a predetermined point in the progression to find an alternative beginning to it.

Example 12.20a.

The bridge of rhythm changes is a series of extended dominant sevenths, generally with an accompanying melodic sequence or with no melody, as in the case of many be-bop rhythm changes tunes.

Example 12.21.

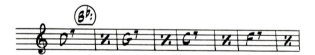

While the obvious reharmonizations suggested by the nature of the progression use substitute dominants and/or the insertion of related II-7 or minor 7(♭5) chords, other modal interchange or cadentially related chords might also be used.

Example 12.22.

In addition, we could reharmonize the bridge, using the standard stride piano cliche reharmonization for bass motion up in fourths (from II-V or between extended dominants as is the case here): I, II-7, #IIo7, III-7.

Example 12.23.

Another alternative to the standard rhythm changes bridge is the chord progression from the bridge to "Eternal Triangle" from the album of the same name featuring Dizzy Gillespie and Sonny Stitt.

Example 12.23a.

Finally, we might arrive at the following generic chart in table 12.1, describing the most common variations possible within the context of the A and B sections of the rhythm changes progression.

Table 12.1. Common Rhythm Changes Variations in B♭.

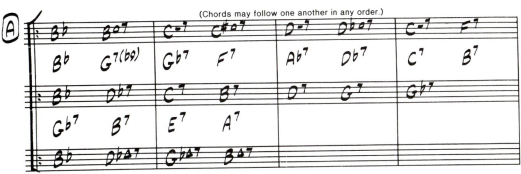

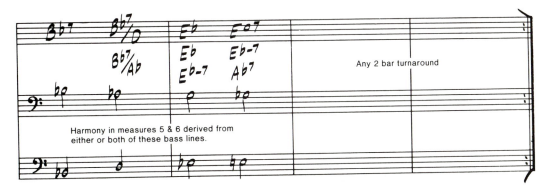

Table 12.1—*Continued*

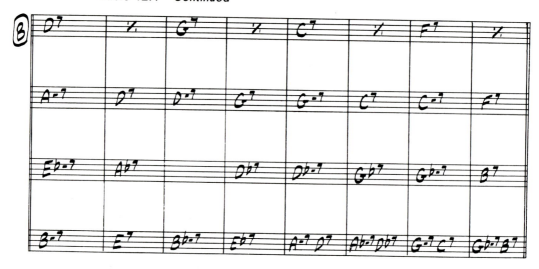

Reharmonization is also one of the most important arranging techniques. For example, we have come to the last eight bars of a chorus of rhythm changes, and we are interested in repeating the same music in the key a tritone away. Exploiting the possibility for substitute dominant root motion, a simple deceptive resolution of any common turnaround would accomplish this.

Example 12.24.

Another effective means of reharmonization is to deliberately manipulate the increasing degree of richness between the melody and the chord. At the same time we attempt to arrive at a functional chord progression, so that we combine all the elements that help to give overall shape to the harmonic phrase. To do this, we first plot out the desired function of each melody note then choose a chord whose function does not hinder the overall direction of the chord progression.

Example 12.25.

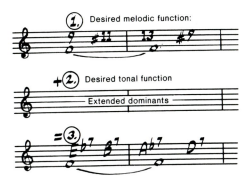

We can intentionally design these reharmonizations that have an inner compositional logic to their structure to make them the selling point of a particular arrangement of a piece. John Coltrane was fond of interpolating his "Giant Steps" or three-tonic system of chord progression into standard II-V-I, four-bar harmonic phrases (see appendices). He either altered the melody to accommodate his new changes or wrote a new one. A good example of the latter procedure is the comparison of Eddie Vinson's composition, "Tune-Up," to what evolved into Coltrane's "Countdown." Another example is 'Trane's arrangement of the Gershwin standard, "But Not For Me," which exploits the relationship between the key centers and the symmetric structure of the whole tone scale (see *example 3.37*).

Example 12.26.

However, not every reharmonization need be so elaborate or compositional in order to succeed. For example, we might simply organize the reharmonization according to a consistent interval between the same type of chord (see chapter 7).

Example 12.27

In conclusion, reharmonization principles are inherently important in composition and in arranging.

One final means of reharmonization, pertaining mainly to arranging, involves deliberate manipulation of tension relationships in a given melody in order to create new harmony. The basic concept involves reharmonizing every note in the melody by making it either a tension or the root or fifth of a chord then filling in the root, third, and seventh below to create harmony. If spacing permits or necessitates additional voices may be added in the form of additional tensions between the upper quality tone and the melody. These new melodic-tension functions, which will dictate the roots of the new chords, may in turn be chosen to create contrapuntal relationships between the bass and the melody.

Example 12.28.

Reharmonization depends upon the player's or writer's awareness of all of the available possibilities, whether through functional replacement of chords, alteration of common turnarounds, enhancement of the level of melodic richness as the chord progression evolves, extraction of counterlines as a source for new harmonies, interpolation of chords, or by structural manipulation of the chord progression. There is always opportunity to present the same melodic fragment or section of the form in a new harmonic context.

---

exercises

Exercise 12.1. Reharmonize the following example as indicated:

Exercise 12.2. Reharmonize the following example. Consult Examples 12.8 through 12.10:

Exercise 12.3. Reharmonize the following rhythm changes chord progression as indicated:

Exercise 12.4. Harmonize the following melody by supplying chords that fulfill the indicated melodic functions:

bibliography for further study

Blesh, Rudi, ed. **Classic Piano Rags.** New York, Dover, 1973.

Markewich, Reese. **Inside Outside: Substitute Harmony in Jazz and Pop Music.** New York: n.p., 1967.

Murphy, Lyle. **Swing Arranging Method.** New York: Robbins Music Corp., 1937.

Nadeau, Roland. "The grace and beauty of classic rags: structural elements in a distinct musical genre." **Ragtimer** (1978): 6-14.

Newberger, Eli. "The development of New Orleans and stride piano styles." **Journal of Jazz Studies** 4 (1977): 43-71.

———. "The transition from ragtime to improvised piano." **Journal of Jazz Studies** 3 (1976): 3-18.

Russo, William. **Composing for the Jazz Orchestra.** Chicago: University of Chicago Press, 1961.

————. **Jazz Composition and Orchestration.** Chicago: University of Chicago Press, 1968.

Sebesky, Don. **The Contemporary Arranger.** Sherman Oaks, CA: Alfred Publishing Co., 1979.

Timothy, Tom. **Modern Arranging.** New York: Charles Colin, 1959.

---

discography for further study

"Countdown." **Giant Steps.** Atlantic SD 1311.

"Eternal Triangle." **Eternal Triangle,** Dizzy Gillepsie and others. Verve Records VRVS2-2505.

"Humph." **Genius of Modern Music: Thelonious Monk., Vol. I.** Blue Note Records BLP1510, BST81510.

"I've Got Rhythm." **Gershwin Songbook,** Ella Fitzgerald. Verve Records VRVS2-2525.

"Rhythm-A-Ning." **Criss-Cross,** Thelonious Monk. Columbia Records LE-10122.

"Tune-Up." **Stanley the Steamer featuring Dexter Grodon,** Stan Levey. Bethlehem Records BCP#-6030.

13 harmony in fourths and other symmetric structures

This chapter examines the means available for expressing the previously discussed chord types in structures built primarily in fourths rather than in thirds. To do this, we begin with a somwhat different scalic source to generate these chords—the *pentatonic scale*. By most standard definitions, a pentatonic scale contains five notes. The most commonly used forms of this scale, however, are the major and minor pentatonic scales, which are related in much the same way as major and minor heptatonic scales. The intervallic formula for the major pentatonic is 1, 2, 3, 5, 6; and the formula for its relative minor pentatonic is 1, ♭3, 4, 5, ♭7 (see chapter 1).

Example 13.1.

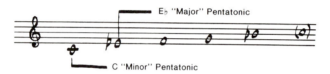

Just as with the chord-scales previously considered, we generate diatonic harmony using these scales. Taking the minor pentatonic as our source and voicing it in a fashion that yields the best overall spacing, we obtain the tonic structure in example 13.2.

Example 13.2.

From looking at this structure we see that it is in itself harmonically ambiguous. After all, the tonic of the scale is not even at the bottom of the voicing. However, we can obtain a wide variety of potential uses for arranging, comping, and improvising on the basis of this structure by finding out exactly how it functions when superimposed on different potential tonics. Doing this systematically is easy enough. We examine the effects of placing each of the different notes in the chromatic scale below this voicing and then treat it as we would any normal chord scale according to the function of each pitch in relation to the new tonic. Example 13.3 examines each pitch in the voicing as it relates to the twelve different possible roots as a chord tone, tension, or mere passing tone. It also analyzes each voicing for harmonic completeness or the lack of it.

Example 13.3.

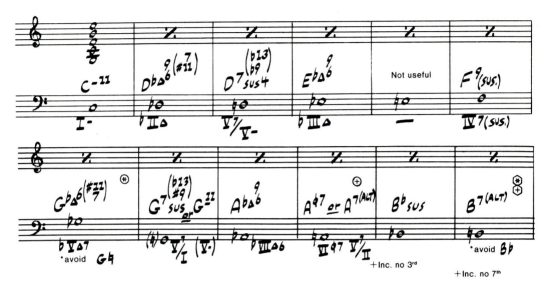

We might group these harmonies according to their respective levels of harmonic completeness and usefulness generally into the following categories:

1. Those that are harmonically complete and in which every note in the voicing sounds consonant with chord

Example 13.4.

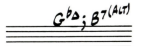

2. Those that are harmonically complete and in which one or more notes in the voicing sound dissonant with the chord (in other words, can have only passing note or appoggiatura function (see appendix 6))

Example 13.5.

3. Those that combine to restrict us to one particular chord scale or mode, yet which present no harmonically complete voicing between them over the given root

Example 13.6.

4. Those that are simply not much use

Example 13.7.

5. Those that are harmonically ambiguous

Example 13.8.

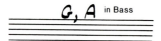

A number of ambiguities surround the use of pentatonics. First, like blues melodies (discussed in chapter 11), they can be used with discretion to enhance the sound of diatonically-related composition or improvisation. They cannot always be counted on to actually constitute a complete tonal system on their own. Second, the minor pentatonic scale might be found in many other scales; this explains its relationship to so many chords that are diatonic to differing primary scalic sources.

Example 13.9.

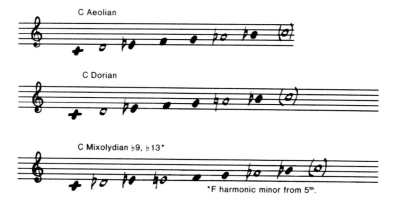

Using ambiguous yet familiar melodies that work equally well in a variety of harmonic situations is very significant. It is sometimes referred to as *pantonality.*

The pentatonic scale is found in many different traditional scale-types. However, the fact that one such scale might generate more than one chord of the same quality implies that any given chord of that particular quality might conversely have as many different parallel scalic sources as the number of occurrences of that chord type within the original pentatonic scale. In other words, if there are four major seventh chords diatonic to a given scale, there must be four different scales of that type that generate a diatonic major seventh chord. In each instance, the function of that major seventh chord within the key center implied by that scale is a bit different.

Example 13.10.

Conversely, the presence of three minor seventh chords in the diatonic scale implies the existence of three associated minor pentatonic scales, which could be employed in diatonic progressions for improvisation.

Example 13.10a.

The next step is to figure out which of the different possible structures in fourths could stand for which parallel structures in thirds, where they might be found, and which possible pentatonic scales generate them and could therefore be used in improvising or writing them. Table 13.1 examines each type of chord structure and the related pentatonic possibilities, as well as how these need to be treated.

Table 13.1.

Chord Type	Possible Pentatonic Scale Sources
Maj⁷	↓m2nd; ↓M3rd; ↓+4th; ↑M3rd
min⁷	Unis; ↓ 1 step; ↓ P4th; ↑P4th;
Sus4(alt)	Unis; ↓ 1 step; ↓ P4th; ↑ P4th; ↑ 1 step
Sus4	↓ 1 step; ↑ P4th
alt. dom. ⁷	↑ m3rd; ↑ ½ step
min⁷(♭5)	↑ m3rd

Learning how to apply these scales for improvisation in a tonal context is extremely valuable. Relating them to the diatonic modes from the major scales they are contained in can provide a means for using them in modal music also (see example 13.11).

Example 13.11.

The uses for the standard pentatonic scale are as varied as those of the blues melodies discussed previously, yet they should not be over used.

Another type of pentatonic scale in common use is the *lydian pentatonic*. This scale melodically represents the arpeggiation of a particularly common left hand voicing used by many pianists. This can have a variety of uses corresponding primarily with its function as a voicing.

Example 13.12.

As with the minor pentatonic and most reharmonization the same voicing can have different harmonic effects depending on what is in the bass below it. Throughout this book we have discussed presenting the identical melodic material in different harmonic contexts as a means of helping to structure composition and improvisation. In this chapter, we have discussed the utility of pentatonic (and blues) scales in this regard. The fact that these scales can be expressed symmetrically plays a large role in assuring their versatility, as does the fact that they contain an unorthodox number of pitches in contrast to the traditional seven-note scales. The same is also true of two of the dominant seventh scales discussed in chapter 6. Because of their symmetric structures they can be used in a variety of parallel harmonic situations: the *symmetric diminished* and *whole-tone* scales.

Only two discrete whole-tone scales exist and either one of them could accommodate six different augmented seventh or dominant seventh (♭13) situations. The whole-tone scale is symmetric with respect to every pitch in it.

Example 13.13.

The same formula results starting from any scaletone.

There are only three discrete symmetric diminished scales; each applies to four different dominant sevenths (altered nine, natural five; see chapter 6) and four diminished sevenths (see chapter 12).

Example 13.14.

A good example of the use of these principles is John Coltrane's arrangement of "But Not For Me," which we referred to when discussing extreme structural reharmonization. As mentioned in the previous chapter (see also example 3.37), in the initial melodic statement of his improvised solo in his arrangement of this piece, Coltrane uses both whole-tone scales concurrently in what might be regarded as an imaginative application of the twelve-tone principle in a jazz context (see appendix 2).

The philosophical point of this chapter is that when nontraditional and symmetric scales are considered, alternatives to the standard voicings in thirds exist. As melodic sources, these scales are not generated by, and therefore restricted to, particular harmonic situations. They should be seen, instead, in terms of the variety of harmonic situations in which they could be applied. Table 13.2 illustrates standard voicings in thirds for the various types of chords, as well as their corresponding primary chord-scales. It presents other alternative voicings and scales that could replace or enhance the more standard options.

Table 13.2.

Chord Type	Standard Scale	Pentatonic Alternatives

exercises

Exercise 13.1. Voice the following pentatonic scale in pure fourths and then indicate what type of chord would be produced if it were played with the indicated pitches in the bass:

Exercise 13.2. Supply the chords on which the following pentatonic scale would fulfill the following functions:

Exercise 13.3. Write out the whole-tone or symmetric diminished scales that relate the following sets of chord symbols:

bibliography for further study

Banacos, Charles. **Pentatonic Scale Improvisation.** Dracut, MA: Charles Banacos Music, 1972.

Bishop, Walter, Jr. **A Study in Fourths.** New York: Caldon Publishing, 1976.

Diorio, Joe. "Melodic continuity using 4ths and 5ths." **Down Beat** 47 (1980): 62–64.

Feather, Leonard. "Piano giants of jazz; McCoy Tyner." **Contemporary Keyboard** 4 (1978): 54–55.

Mehegan, John. "Contemporary Piano Styles." **Jazz Improvisation.** Vol. 4. New York: Watson-Guptill, 1965.

Ricker, Ramon. **Pentatonic Scales for Jazz Improvisation.** Lebanon, IN: Studio P/R, 1975.

————. **Technique Development in Fourths.** Lebanon, IN: Studio P/R, 1976.

discrograph for further study

"Jinrikisha." **Joe Henderson Page One.** Blue Note 84140.

further considerations in modal harmony and chord substitution: miscellaneous considerations in arranging

14

We discuss the concepts in this chapter in order to broaden our perspectives on the uses of harmony in creating music in the various contemporary jazz styles. Conversely, we intend to show what effects different stylistic approaches to musical construction might have upon the use of harmony itself.

The Modal Style

The modal style of jazz evolved in the late '50s and early '60s; among its best known creators are Miles Davis and John Coltrane. Its characteristics are (1) relative simplicity of harmonic activity when compared with earlier jazz styles, be-bop in particular, (2) relative sparseness and rhythmic unpredictabiliity of melodic activity in contrast to those same styles, and (3) treatment of dissonance in a new perspective, especially as it relates to the emphasis placed upon particularly distinctive pitches within each mode.

The last characteristic most clearly affects considerations of harmony. Each chord in a modal progression (or section of a piece) is made to last longer, thereby decreasing its function within any parent tonality and giving more the impression of its constituting its own, very strong temporary tonality. In terms of actual chord voicings, it is important to include within the chord itself (or melody within the duration of that chord) that pitch, or combination of pitches, that distinguishes the given mode from other parallel modalities on the same root with which it might otherwise be confused. Another way of looking at this problem is to create simple modal cadences that vamp back and forth between chords containing those notes distinctive to the given mode and the tonic (I) chord, especially in modes where those pitches are not contained in the normal configuration of that tonic chord. Substitution for the tonic chord is not possible in a modal context.

This first group of cadences in example 14.1 shows that latter procedure in action.

Example 14.1.

Contrast these examples with the chord voicings shown below, in which traditional concepts of "wrong" notes on particular types of chords have been abandoned in order to create relatively more dissonant modal voicings that yield a very distinctive modal coloration.

Example 14.2.

Finally, we can create chords that are modal in flavor by arbitrarily superimposing diatonic harmonies from the mode on the root of the mode. We can consider the extensions of a given chord to have been voiced above the root without one or both of the normally intervening quality tones being present.

Example 14.3.

Notice that some of the sonorities in this example sound relatively more or less consonant in relation to the root of the mode than do others. This is due to the fact that some of the chords superimposed above the modal root relate to it as possible extensions without the complete chord quality being present, whereas others have no such logically implied relationship to rely upon. Since the characteristic note of the given mode is probably present in such a sonority, the resulting sound is quite dissonant. Compare the following voicings in example 14.4.

Example 14.4.

Notice that it is still ultimately the original relationship to tonality that yielded the extraction of the mode and its harmony.

Example 14.5.

The next step is to calculate all the possible polychordal structures that can be derived from the diatonic and other modes studied to this point. Table 14.1 lists the most commonly emloyed triadic and seventh chord extensions created in this manner. The possibilities inherent in the diatonic modes directly relate to the diatonic modal harmony discussed in chapter 8.

Table 14.1. Triadic and Seventh Chord Extensions.

Many interesting *polymodal* or *hybrid* chord structures may be created from the distinctive intervallic combinations made possible through the use of different scales. These structures represent more ambiguous alternatives to traditional, harmonically complete, chord voicings and are interesting to listen to precisely because of this ambiguity.

Table 14.2. Common Hybrid Chords and Their Derivations.

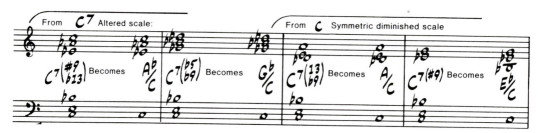

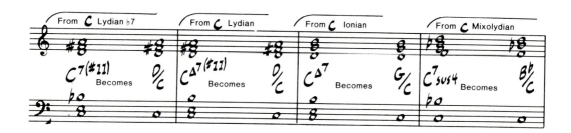

These types of voicings may be combined in cadences, which might be derived by harmonizing a given melodic fragment triadically and placing it above a contrary motion bass line.

Example 14.5a.

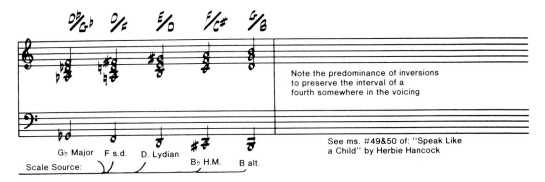

Note the predominance of inversions to preserve the interval of a fourth somewhere in the voicing

Scale Source: Gb Major   F s.d.   D. Lydian   Bb H.M.   B alt.

See ms. #49&50 of: "Speak Like a Child" by Herbie Hancock

This approach to chord scales gives rise to an alternative method of perceiving them. Instead of thinking in terms of a scale, the improvisor can think of the various harmonies that are diatonic to that scale. In this manner the improvisor may learn substitute harmonies that enable adoption of a more harmonic, and less scalar concept of improvisation, avoiding the danger of merely playing scales during a solo. To take an example of this concept at work, we can think of a G7 (altered) chord as a combination of an Ab-6 chord, a Gϕ7 chord, a Bb-7 chord, and an Eb7 chord, to name just a few of the diatonic seventh chords available in the altered scale.

Example 14.5b.

Table 14.2a lists some traditional chord scales and their related diatonic harmony. These seventh chords can be combined to create substitue progressions for use in improvisation in lieu of the traditional chord scale approach.

Table 14.2a. Standard Chord Substitutions.

Scale   **Substitute Chords**

Table 14.2a.—*Continued*

Scale   **Substitute Chords**

. . . any other diatonically-derived harmony.

exercises

Exercise 14.1. Label and analyze the following modal voicings. Assume that the bass note is the tonic note of the chord:

bibliography for further study

The Arrangers' Dreambook. 2 vols. N.p.: J.D. Music Publications, 1976.

Baker, David. **Arranging and Composing for the Small Ensemble: Jazz/R & B/ Jazz-Rock.** Chicago: Maher Publications, 1970.

————. "Bibliography of compositions containing examples of modes and scales." **Advanced Improvisation.** Chicago: Maher Publications, 1974.

Budds, Michael. **Jazz in the Sixties; the Expansion of Musical Sources and Techniques.** Iowa City, IA: University of Iowa Press, 1978.

Chasman, Paul. "Five steps in arranging." **Frets** 2 (1980): 48–49.

de Rose, Nino. "Il jazz modale." **Musica Jazz** 36 (1980): 2–6.

Delamont, Gordon. **Modern Arranging and Composing.** Delevan, NY: Kendor Music, 1965.

————. **Modern Arranging Technique.** Delevan, NY: Kendor Music, 1966.

————. **Modern Harmonic Technique.** 2 vols. Delevan, NY: Kendor Music, 1965.

————.. "The nature of arranging." **Canadian Musician** 1 (1979): 34–35, 45–47.

Dellaira, Angelo. **Creative Arranging: New Sounds in Modern Music.** New York: Charles Colin, 1966.

Delp, Ron. "Contemporary harmony: arranging; harmonizing a melody." **Musician, Player & Listener** 22–27 (1980): 82, 90, 96, 110.

————. "Contemporary harmony: so you want to be an arranger." **Musician, Player & Listener** 16 (1979): 70.

Ellis, Norman. **Instrumentation and Arranging for the Radio and Dance Orchestra.** New York: Roell, 1936.

Garcia, Russell. **The Professional Arranger Composer.** New York: Criterion, 1954.

Kumpf, Hans. "Jazz und Avantgarde." **Musik und Bildung** 9 (1977): 521–525.

Kuzmich, John, Jr. "Combo charts: an update." **The Instrumentalist** 31 (1977): 61–63.

LaPorta, John. **Functional Piano for the Improvisor.** Delevan, NY: Kendor Music, 1969.

Mancini, Henry. **Sounds and Scores.** N.p.: Northridge Music, 1973.

Murphy, Lyle. **Swing Arranging Method.** New York: Robbins Music Corp., 1937.

"Pete Rugolo talks to Howard Lucraft about arranging." **Jazz Journal International** 33 (1980): 14.

Russo, William. **Composing for the Jazz Orchestra.** Chicago: University of Chicago Press, 1961.

————. **Jazz Composition and Orchestration.** Chicago: University of Chicago Press, 1968.

Sebesky, Don. **The Contemporary Arranger.** Sherman Oaks, CA: Alfred Publishing Co., 1979.

Smith, John. "Form analysis for jazz arrangers." **Music Educators Journal** 66 (1980): 36–37.

Stuart, Walter. **The Chord Approach to Improvising.** New York: Charles Colin, 1966.

Taylor, Billy. "Jazz improvisation: voicings for large hands." **Contemporary Keyboard** 5 (1979): 91.

Timothy, Tom. **Modern Arranging.** New York: Charles Colin, 1959.

Welburn, Ron. "Some limits to modal improvising today: the Sonny Rollins example." **The Grackle** 5 (1979): 22–24.

---

discography for further study

"Speak Like A Child." **Speak Like A Child.** Blue Note 84279.

appendixes

---

appendix 1   analysis of "giant steps" by john coltrane

A. Motivic Analysis

Example A1.1.

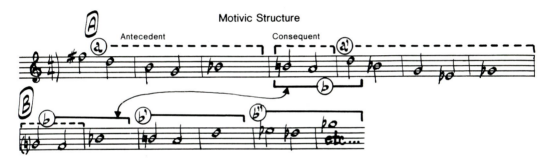

This piece contains two main phrases; one is four bars long and repeated (measures 1–4, 5–8), and the other is composed of a primary idea (measures 1–3) and a secondary idea (measure 4). It is this second idea that is extracted in combination with what would be the initial note of a third repetition of A to create B (measures 8 and 9). Due to this melodic elision we hear the structure of this melody as follows in example A1.2.

Example A1.2.

Measure #'s:	Motivic Event
1 - 4	A (=a(1−3)+b(4))
5 - 8	Sequence of A
8 - 9	B (=meas. 4+5 extracted and transposed)
10 - 15	Sequential repetitions of B
16	Harmonic turnaround

B. Harmonic Analysis

Example A1.3.

Harmonic Structure

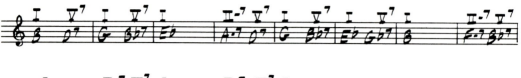

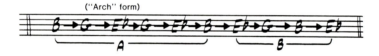

Each of the two phrases (see part A) in the first section of this piece is comprised of three direct modulations. The B section of each of these phrases (measures 4, 8) contains a II–V cadence; the second (see part A, again) begins a series of harmonic sequences through the series of keys established in the A section. The series of keys is not the same throughout, although the keys themselves are.

Example A1.4.

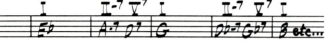

Since this piece begins and ends in B, we hear it as the primary key center. Actually the three keys are all equal in strength, and these symmetric key relationships, whose roots combine to spell an augmented triad, achieved nearly symbolic significance in Coltrane's music (see appendix 2).

C. Pitch Analysis

There is one more aspect to the construction of this deceptively simple, yet uniquely styled and inspiring piece of music that transcends even the control exerted in its melodic and harmonic form. If we were to take all of the distinct pitches contained in each of the two phrases discussed in part A, we would obtain the following two sets of pitches.

Example A1.5.

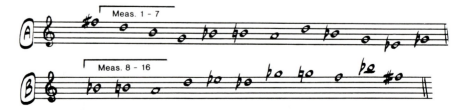

We can then further reduce these lists by eliminating all of the repeated pitches.

Example A1.6.

With these two sets of pitches as a point of reference, we can then discover the significance of those left out of each phrase. In measures 1–7, the five pitches in example A1.7 are left over.

Example A1.7.

In measures 8–16, these three pitches remain unstated.

Example A1.8.

Truly, "Giant Steps" represents musical architecture and genius of the highest order.

Discography

"Giant Steps." **Giant Steps.** Atlantic SD 1311.

---

appendix 2   analysis of reharmonization of "but not for me" arranged by john coltrane

A.

Example A2.1.

In his classic reharmonization, Coltrane interpolates three direct modulations within this same phrase.

B.

Example A2.2.

In the process, a descending whole-tone scale appears in the bass, alternating between the roots of the new I chords and the fifths of their respective dominants. Note the similarity of key relationships with "Giant Steps" (appendix 1). However, in this case the process continues one step further and thus permits the return to the original key—a fact that enabled Coltrane to substitute this progression at will (either with or without the rhythm section) wherever the standard 4-bar II-V-I phrase occurred. As mentioned in chapter 12, example 12.8, this technique is applied in "Countdown," compared with its progenitor "Tune-Up," and can be seen at work in many of Coltrane's improvisations, as in example A2.3.

Example A2.3.

Beginning of Coltrane's Solo or But Not For Me (See Ex 3.37)

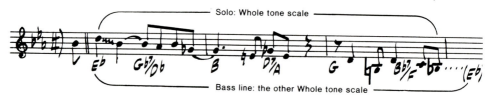

C. Let's return briefly to the significance of the use of the whole-tone scale in the bass in example A2.3. Just as its presence in the bass lends organization to the arrangement, that presence implies the use of the other whole-tone scale as a basis for improvisation on these reharmonized chords. This is because the dominant chords in these three interpolated keys (as would three others) all could accommodate the same whole-tone scale as a source of chord tones and available tensions. This is due to the symmetric nature of the scale (see chapters 6, 13).

Example A2.4.

Interpolating these key relationships requires drastic melodic alteration (compare published sheet music of "But Not For Me" with Coltrane's version of the melody— it is barely recognizable during the first eight bars). Therefore, a closer look at these newly created key relationships enabled Coltrane to come up with yet another, although totally different, approach to the employment of all twelve tones in close proximity to one another as a means of compositional organization. In "Giant Steps" this was accomplished by omission; in "But Not For Me" the concept revolves around the coexistence of the two discrete whole-tone scales— one as a source of melodic organization and one as a means of harmonic organization (refer again to example 3.37).

We can see that the applications of the principles of symmetry and what might more traditionally have been called atonality in the work of John Coltrane are indeed imaginative.

Bibliography

Baker, David. "Woodwinds: Analysis of the music of John Coltrane." **Down Beat** 46 (1979): 70–72.

Buhles, Gunter. "Atonalitat und Jazz." **HiFi Stereophonie** 18 (1979): 1732–1738.

Cole, William S. "The Style of John Coltrane, 1955–1967." Ph.D dissertation, Wesleyan University, 1975.

Liebman, David. "A look at John Coltrane groups." **NAJE Educator** 11 (1979): 14–16, 52–54.

White, Andrew. **Trane 'n Me.** Washington, D.C.: Andrew's Music, 1981.

———. **The Works of John Coltrane.** 10 vols. Washington, D.C.: Andrew's Musical Enterprises, n.d.

Discography

"But Not For Me." **My Favorite Things.** Atlantic 1361.

appendix 3 "chelsea bridge" by billy strayhorn

The following composition is included for purposes of harmonic analysis since it includes examples of each type of modulation as well as differing means of accomplishing them.

Example A3.1.

"Chelsea Bridge"—Strayhorn

Discography

"Chelsea Bridge." **Ellington Songbook.** Verve VE–Z–2535.

appendix 3a   "daahoud" by clifford brown

Another interesting example for studying the use of modulation is Clifford Brown's "Daahoud." Notice that in the A sections the melodic tonal center never seems to vary from E♭ (employing parallel major and minor pentatonic scales melodically) while the harmonic key centers do change. This is an example of the pantonal possibilities of the pentatonic scale (see chapter 13). In the bridge, the melody also seems to have a different tonal center than the harmony if the two are played separately.

Example A3a.1.

Discography
"Daahoud." **Daahoud.** Mainstream MRL 386.

appendix 4
motivic analysis of "the keeper" by andy jaffe

Example A4.1.

"The Keeper"—A. Jaffe

⊛ = $B^{7(\#11)}$ NO 3rd

Example A4.1A

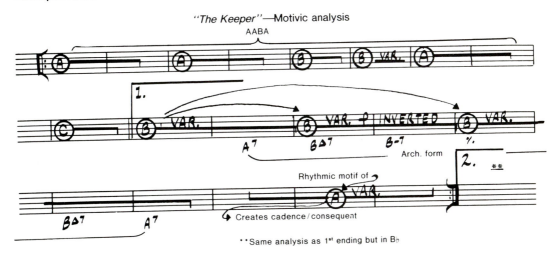

"The Keeper"—Motivic analysis

AABA

Arch. form

Rhythmic motif of

Creates cadence/consequent

**Same analysis as 1st ending but in B♭

Notice that those methods of development normally applied to melodic ideas might also be applied to chord progressions (see measures 11 and 12, then 15 and 16). Also notice the concept of creating new melodic material by introducing the new idea which is subsequently combined with the old. For example, measure 9 is entirely new, whereas the second part of its phrase, measure 10, is familiar. The point is that infinite development is possible in the context of the melodic development in each component—rhythmic, melodic, harmonic—of a given idea. These components have their own potential melodic integrity independently of the others.

Incidentally, we refer to the motivic/harmonic device used here as *constant structure*. (See chapter 7.)

Example A4.2.

C Dorian   D♭ Dorian   A⁷   D⁷   G♭⁷   F⁷   E°⁷

In other words, there is one basic harmonic structure (a tritone supporting a perfect fourth, intervallically) that, in various transpositions and with differing relationships to these successive bass notes, generates all of the harmonies in this piece. This has the effect of making it sound very modal.

Bibliography

Buhles, Günter. "Thelonius Monk: jazz composer." **Jazz Podium**. 27 (1978): 4–9.

appendix 5 reharmonization of "my one and only love"

The following example, a reharmonized version of the last eight bars of "My One and Only Love," illustrates various concepts in reharmonization.

Example A5.1.

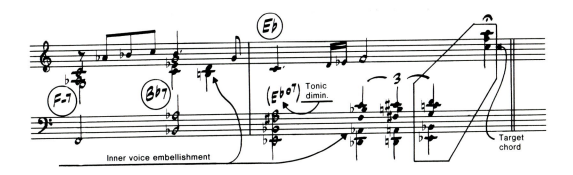

The principles shown above are the following:

1. Original harmony maintained at point of original chord changes with re-harmonization between
2. Reharmonization generated by original chord scales, derived from original changes
3. Sequences created wherever possible in reharmonization to accompany those in melody and thereby reinforce structure and coherence of chord progression

appendix 6 summary of the most common generic chord scales by chord type

Example A6.1.

Example A6.1—Continued

The value of generic chord scales is that they enable one to play without creating a wrong note. Notice that every pitch listed above has some harmonic function associated with it.

As for the triads, see how they are used in the examples from appendix 7 and how those relate to the above chord scales.

Bibliography

Watson, Robert. "Arranging and composing for the Jazz Messengers." **Down Beat** 46 (1979): 90.

Williams, James. "How to write for the Jazz Messengers." **Down Beat** 46 (1979): 89.

appendix 7   standard chord voicings for arranging

This list could not possibly be exhaustive. It is intended to show several possibilities available to the arranger seeking to express a given harmony with a certain number of voices available. Some show complete chord quality; others opt for certain interval configurations.

A. Three-Part

Example A7.1.

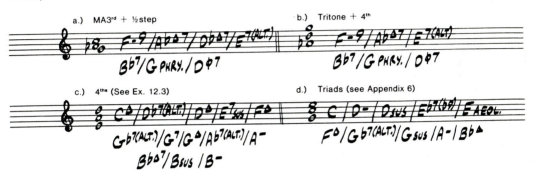

B. Four-Part

Example A7.2.

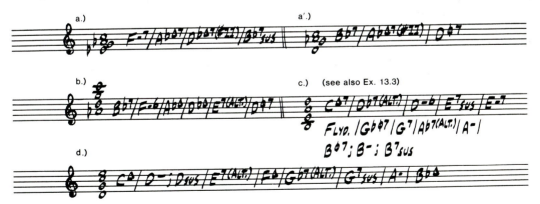

C. Five- and Six-Part

Example A7.3.

Regardless of instrumentation, it is important when scoring the above voicings to understand a few simple assumptions:

1. The root need not be included in the voicing. We assume that the rhythm section will take care of that. For similar reasons, certain of these voicings seem to be harmonically incomplete. Which are they? Of the incomplete voicings, (for example, missing the third or seventh, or possibly both,) which successfully convey the sound of the chord in spite the absent chord tone(s)? How does a particular combination of tensions used above a given root imply a given chord quality with or without its actual complete presence (see appendix 6)?

2. Certain extensions from a given chord scale might be used in one voicing in the inner voices and avoided in another. What are the generalities that determine the availability of particular inner voices below given melodic functions?

3. With the notable exception of the *clusters,* * most of these voicings are open voicings. This alignment yields more interesting intervallic construction than the predictable traditional use of thirds predominantly.

4. Tensions are generally voiced above chord tones if possible. This not only corresponds to their normal hierarchy within the overtone series, it also avoids many vertical problems in the inner voices referred to above.

In any event, they are generally not voiced below ![music symbol], to avoid muddiness. Their availability, as well as that of every other note used in a given voicing, is determined by the chord scale from which the voicing is derived (see appendix 6).

Bibliography

Schaeffer, Don, and Colin, Charles. **Encyclopedia of Scales.** New York: New Sounds in Modern Music, 1964.

Slonimsky, Nicolas. **Thesaurus of Scales and Melodic Patterns.** New York: Charles Scribner's Sons, 1947.

Wyble, Jimmy. ''Combining scales to expand technique and harmonic awareness.'' **Guitar Player** 13 (1979): 82.

---

appendix 8   standard chord symbols

The following is a list of most of the commonly used chord symbols you will encounter in jazz music.

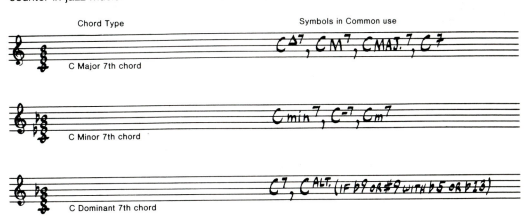

*Voicings in seconds

C Major 6th chord — C^6, CM^6

C Minor 6th chord — C^{-6}, Cm^6

C Minor/Major 7th chord — $C^{-\triangle 7}$, $Cmin/MAJ.^7$, $C^{-}MAJ^7$

C Augmented 7th chord — C^{+7}, $CAUG.^7$

C Diminished 7th chord — C^{o7}, $Cdim^7$

C Augmented Major 7th chord — $C^{+\triangle 7}$, $CAUG. MAJ.^7$

C Minor seven, flat five chord — $C^{-7(b5)}$, $C^{\emptyset 7}$

Bibliography

Brandt, Carl, and Roemer, Clinton. **Standardized Chord Symbol Notation.** Sherman Oaks, CA: Roerick Music, 1976.

glossary

Aeolian—(also known as natural or pure minor)—sixth mode of the major scale

Altered scale—(also known as the superlocrian scale)—seventh mode of the melodic minor scale

Altered seventh chord—dominant seventh chord with one or more altered tensions either replacing the root and/or the fifth of the chord, or voiced as extensions above the basic seventh chord

Altered tensions—tensions associated with the altered scale (♭9,♯9,♭5,♭13)

Antecedent phrase—a melodic phrase that seems incomplete by itself

Anticipation—syncopation created by the forward displacement of a rhythmic attack, usually by one half beat

Augmentation—presentation of a melodic motif in larger rhythmic note values

Augmented major seventh chord—seventh chord obtained by superimposing an interval of a minor third above an augmented triad in root position

Augmented seventh chord—seventh chord obtained by superimposing an interval of a whole step above an augmented triad in root position

Augmented triad—triad created by superposition of two major third intervals above the root

Be-bop—the classical jazz style, epitomized by the music of the mid-1940s through the mid-1950s as created by such musicians as Charlie Parker, Dizzy Gillespie, Max Roach, Bud Powell, and Thelonious Monk

Blue notes—specific nondiatonic notes, which, when superimposed on basic triadic harmony (usually in the form of simple chorale-style cadences), create blues harmony and melody (Most commonly these are the flatted third, fifth and seventh of the key.)

Blues—category of harmonic progression and its associated derivative musical style, usually twelve bars in length, featuring two phrases in the first eight bars and a final four bar consequent phrase which includes a cadence

Blues harmony—harmony characteristic of the blues form, created by the superposition of blues notes on diatonic harmony (Common examples are the I7 chord, the IV7 chord, the I7(♯9) chord, and the V7(♭13,♯9) chord.)

Bossa nova—Latin dance style featuring the following repeating syncopated rhythmic figure:

Bridge (also known as the channel)—middle and contrasting part of the form of a tune, found between an A section and the final repetition of the A section or something closely related to it

Cadence—harmonic movement from unstable harmony to stable harmony

Characteristic chords—harmony that distinguishes a given mode from other parallel modal forms

Characteristic notes—pitch or pitches that distinguish a given mode from other parallel forms

Chord—vertical coincidence of more than two notes

Chord progression—movement from one harmony to another

Chord scale—scale associated with a particular chord for use in creating improvisation or harmonic extensions, usually associated with the chord's function within the key

Chromatic scale—scale produced by playing all twelve distinct pitches in adjacent order

Common tones—pitches common to adjacent chords in a progression

Compound interval—intervals larger than one octave (ninths, tenths, etc.)

Consequent phrase—a melodic phrase that completes, or answers, an antecedent one

Consonance—perceived harmonic or melodic stability

Contour—melodic shape

Constant structure—process of transposing a type of chord or a simple two-chord progression in sequence (without regard to harmonic function) as a means of generating chord progression

Deceptive resolution—chord progression that results from a dominant seventh chord being followed by something other than its expected or implied target

Development—process of creating more melodic material from an existing motif, usually by alteration of its rhythmic content/placement, or melodic contour

Diatonic—of or pertaining to the scale, usually understood to mean the major scale

Diatonic modes—scales produced by shifting the root of the major scale to each of its individual pitches

Diminished seventh chord—seventh chord produced by superimposing an interval of another minor third above a diminished triad in root position

Diminished triad—triad created by superposition of two minor third intervals above the root

Diminution—presentation of a motif in smaller rhythmic note values

Displacement—repetition of a motif at a point within the phrase which receives a different rhythmic stress than did its original presentation

Dissonance—perceived harmonic or melodic instability

Dominant chord—chord containing the fourth and seventh scale degrees of the diatonic tonality within which it is functioning (V7 and VIIφ7)

Dominant seventh chord—seventh chord obtained by superimposing an interval of a minor third above a major triad in root position

Dorian—second mode of the major scale

Elision—overlap of two melodic or harmonic phrases so that the end of the first is also the beginning of the next

Embellishment—decoration, usually melodic, of a basic harmonic progression or melodic motif

Enharmonic(s)—phenomenon of two different names for the same pitch or chord (for example, D♯-E♭)

Enharmonic spelling—use of either of two enharmonic equivalents in describing a pitch or chord

Extended dominant(s)—dominant seventh chords resolving in a "chainlike" manner to other dominant sevenths rather than to expected diatonic targets

Fifth—note found above the third (and below the seventh, if one exists) of a root position triad or seventh chord

First inversion—arrangement of a triad or seventh chord in which the third is the lowest note

Fragmentation—breaking a melodic phrase or motif down into smaller units for separate use in development

-H-

Harmonic minor scale—scale made up of the interval formula: 1,½,1,1,½,+2nd,½

Hi-hat (also known as sock cymbal)—two small cymbals placed opposite one another on a stand so that they may be opened and closed with the drummer's foot, usually on the second and fourth beats of a 4/4 measure

Hybrid chord—harmony that results when a triad or seventh chord is played above an unrelated bass note

-I-

Interpolation—process of adding chords to a pre-existing progression, usually by inserting them before chords to which they are cadentially related

Interval—distance in pitch between two different notes

Inversion (harmonic)—reversal of intervallic relationships between two pitches or between all the pitches contained within a chord, produced by maintaining the upper pitch or pitches in stationary position while moving the lowest one up an octave

Inversion (motivic)—presentation of a motif upside down

-J-

Jazz eighths—eighth notes as played in most jazz music, in which the first of a group receives greater rhythmic stress than the second

-K-

Key-of-the-moment (also known as temporary key)—temporary illusion of tonality produced by preceding a diatonic chord by its secondary dominant

-L-

Latin rhythm(s)—rhythmic patterns characteristic of the musical styles found in the Caribbean and South America, generally featuring syncopations which are typical of jazz played with straight (not swing) eighth notes. Examples of related dance styles would be the bossa-nova, samba, and mambo

Leading tone—seventh degree of the major scale

Lead sheet—sheet music containing melody and unrealized chord changes

Locrian—seventh mode of the major scale

Lydian—fourth mode of the major scale

Lydian augmented scale—third mode of the melodic minor scale

Lydian flat seven scale (also known as mixolydian flat-five scale)—fourth mode of the melodic minor scale

-M-

Major scale (also known as ionian mode)—scale with the interval formula: 1,1,½,1,1,1,½

Major seventh chord—seventh chord obtained by superimposing an interval of a major third above a major triad in root position

Major sixth chord—chord created by superimposing an interval of a whole step above a major triad in root position

Major triad—triad obtained from the root position formula of a major third beneath a minor third

Melodic minor (also known as jazz minor)—scale made up of the intervallic formula: 1,½,1,1,1,1,½

Minor key—key in which the tonic chord is minor in quality

Minor major seventh chord—seventh chord obtained by superimposing an interval of a major third above a minor triad in root position

Minor-seven-flat-five chord (also known as the half-diminished seventh chord)—seventh chord created by superimposing an interval of a major third above a diminished triad in root position

Minor seventh chord—seventh chord obtained by superimposing an interval of a minor third above a minor triad in root position

Minor sixth chord—chord created by superimposing an interval of a whole step above a minor triad in root position

Minor triad—triad obtained from the root position formula of a minor third beneath a major third

Mixolydian—fifth mode of the major scale

Mixolydian ♭13 scale—fifth mode of the melodic minor scale

Mixolydian ♭9,♭13 scale—fifth mode of the harmonic minor scale

Modal chord progression—simple, repetitive chord progression that attempts to establish the root of one of the related diatonic modes (other than ionian) as the tonal center

Modal interchange—process of borrowing harmony from parallel modes for use in the ionian mode

Modal music—music featuring melody and harmony that is characteristic of individual diatonic modes other than ionian

Mode—variation of a scale produced by shifting its tonal center to a different degree of the scale

Modulation—long lasting change of key

Motif—basic melodic idea or germ out of which larger phrases or sections of a piece are developed

—*N*~ **Natural tensions**—tensions associated with the lydian or lydian-flat seven scale (9,♯11,13)

Nondiatonic—not belonging to the (ionian) scale

Nonfunctional harmony—chords (most commonly dominant sevenths) used in ways contrary to their normal or common functions in the key

- *O* - **Octave**—interval of twelve semitones, the distance from a given pitch to the next highest or lowest repetition of that pitch

Open position (chords)—chords in which the normal hierarchy of root, third, fifth, seventh is disturbed

- *p* - **Pantonality**—property of a melodic fragment or type of scale (particularly pentatonic scales) that enables it to be used in more than one key without alteration

Parallel mode(s)—modes of different quality based on the same root

Passing diminished seventh—diminished seventh chord situated between two diatonic chords (or two chords with diatonic roots) which are usually a step apart

Passing tones—pitches in a melodic passage that are not related to the harmony of the passage

Pentatonic harmony—harmony derived from the pentatonic scale

Pentatonic scale(s)—scales of five notes, most commonly these consist of the interval formula: m3,1,1,m3,1; or its relative major pentatonic scale: 1,1,m3,1,m3

Phrygian—third mode of the major scale

Pivot modulation—modulation in which one or more chords are shared by both the old and the new keys

Polychord—chord composed of one recognizable triad or seventh chord superimposed upon or interlocking with another

Polyrhythms—process of playing more than one meter at once, usually with reference to a common downbeat

- *Q* - **Quality tones** (also known as guide tones)—those pitches that, when combined with the chord's root, create the essential sound of the chord (Most commonly these are the third and sixth or seventh of the chord, unless the fifth of the chord is of an altered type, as in a diminished seventh.)

Quartal harmony—harmony based primarily on the interval of a fourth

—*R*- **Reharmonization**—rewriting of a chord progression with the purposes of creating richer and more interesting vertical relationships between the melody and its associated harmony, as well as improvement in the horizontal movement of the chord progression itself

Related minor seventh—minor seventh found a perfect fourth beneath a dominant seventh, combined with which it would create a two-five

Related modes—modes containing the same notes, but with different tonal centers

Resolution—chord progression from a dominant seventh chord to any succeeding chord, usually a chord with a root found a perfect fifth or a half step lower

Retrograde—presentation of a motif backwards

Retrograde inversion—presentation of a motif upside down and backwards

Rhythm changes—chord progression to Gershwin's "I've Got Rhythm," and its many variations

Root—note after which a chord is named (for example, C is the root of C7.)

Root position—arrangement of a chord voiced in such a manner that the root is in the lowest voice

Salsa—Latin dance and instrumental style characterized by the predominance of quarter note anticipations in the bass

Scale—linear expression of specific stepwise interval combinations

Secondary dominant—dominant seventh chords found a perfect fifth above diatonic chords other than I or VII

Second inversion—arrangement of a chord voiced in such a manner that the fifth is in the lowest voice

Sequence—repetition of a melodic, rhythmic, or harmonic idea at a different pitch level or a different point in the phrase

Seventh—note found above the fifth and below the root in a root position seventh chord

Seventh chord(s)—four-note chords built in thirds

Subdominant chord(s)—chords containing the fourth but not the seventh degrees of the major scale

Subdominant minor chords—category of harmony, primarily diatonic to the natural minor scale, that contains the flatted sixth degree of the scale and that is most commonly used as a source of modal interchange harmony (These chords are: bIIMA7, IIø7, IV-6 or 7, bVIMA7, and bVII7.)

Substitute dominant(s)—dominant seventh chords found a tritone distant from one another and that share the same tritone

Symmetric diminished scale—scale used on dominant seventh (b9) chords and diminished seventh chords, with the formula: 1,½,1,½,1,½,1,½ or ½,1,½,1,½,1,½,1

Syncopation—displacement, usually forward, of on-the-beat attacks to a position off the beat to produce a different type of accent throughout the duration of an entire phrase.

Synthetic scale—scale made up of parts of pre-existing scales which is not in itself a mode of any other scale

Tension(s) (also known as extensions)—tertial additions to seventh chords by which five-, six-, and seven-note chords may be obtained (described as ninths, elevenths, and thirteenths, respectively)

Third—note found between the root and the fifth in a root position chord

Third inversion—inversion of a seventh chord in which the seventh of the chord is in the lowest voice

Three-tonic-system—system of tonal organization in which not one, but three tonal centers exist, each of equal weight, and making the outline of an augmented triad (John Coltrane is its most celebrated exponent.)

Tonic chord(s)—chord(s) that are neither subdominant nor dominant, yet which are diatonic (I, III- and VI-)

Tonicization (also known as key-of-the-moment)—process of creating a key-of-the-moment, as opposed to a modulation

Transitional modulation—modulation in which a series of chords, usually in some sort of sequence, is used as a bridge between keys but is not perceived as belonging to either harmonically

Transposition—moving a melody or chord to another pitch level, usually to accommodate its performance on a transposing instrument

Triad(s)—three-note chords in thirds

Tritone—(1) distance (interval) of one-half an octave (six semitones) and (2) third and seventh of a dominant seventh chord

Turnaround—simple, often repeating, progression, usually involving three or four chords, that has the effect of reinforcing the tonic chord by moving slightly away from it and then implying a resolution to it; often used as the harmonic basis for improvised introductions and endings

Two-five—cadence from a minor seventh chord to a dominant seventh chord whose root is a perfect fourth higher

Vamp—simple repetitive chord progression

Voice-leading—efficient movement between adjacent chords that is produced by retention of common tones wherever possible (and observing stepwise motion of the other voices)

Whole-tone scale—synthetic scale with the formula: 1,1,1,1,1,1

recommended discography

The Bass. 3-Impulse 9284.

The Drums. 3-Impulse 9272.

Folkways Jazz. 11 vols. Folkways FJ 2801–2811.

Giants of Jazz. Time-Life Recordings STL 901-.

Jazz Piano Anthology. 2-Columbia PG 32355.

The Saxophone. 3-Impulse 9253.

Smithsonian Collection of Classic Jazz. Columbia P6 11891.

bibliography

Baker, David. **Advanced Ear Training for Jazz Musicians.** Lebanon, IN: Studio P/R, 1977.

————. **Advanced Improvisation.** Chicago: Maher Publications, 1974.

————. **David Baker Monograph Series.** New York: Hansen Publications, 1976.

————. **Jazz Improvisation.** Chicago: Maher Publications, 1973.

Barr, Walter L. "The Jazz Studies Curriculum." Ed.D. dissertation, Arizona State University, 1974.

Baudoin, Philippe. "Compositions de Charlie Parker." **Jazzophone** 1 (1978): 21–22.

Buhles, Günter. "Thelonius Monk: jazz composer." **Jazz Podium** 27 (1978): 4–9.

Coker, Jerry. **Improvising Jazz.** Englewood Cliffs, NJ: Prentice-Hall, 1964.

————. **The Jazz Idiom.** Englewood Cliffs, NJ: Prentice-Hall, 1975.

————. **Listening to Jazz.** Englewood Cliffs, NJ: Prentice-Hall, 1978.

Coker, Jerry; Casale, James; Campbell, Gary; and Greene, Jerry. **Patterns For Jazz.** Lebanon, IN: Studio P/R, 1970.

Collier, James Lincoln. **The Making of Jazz: A Comprehensive History.** Boston: Houghton Mifflin, 1978.

Copeland, Ray. **The Ray Copeland Method: An Approach to the Art of Jazz Improvisation.** New York: Bill Hanson, 1974.

Damron, Bert L., Jr. "The Developmment and Evaluation of a Self-Instructional Sequence in Jazz Improvisation." Ph.D. dissertation, Florida State University, 1973.

Dankeworth, Avril. **Jazz: An Introduction to Its Musical Basis.** London: Oxford University Press, 1968.

Davis, Nathan T. "The Early Life and Music of Charlie Parker." Ph.D. dissertation, Wesleyan University, 1974.

Delamont, Gordon. **Modern Melodic Technique.** Delevan, NY: Kendor Music, 1976.

Dobbins, Bill. **The Contemporary Jazz Pianist.** 4 vols. Jamestown, RI: GAMT Music Press, 1978.

Encyclopedia of Improvisation. New York: Charles Colin, 1972.

Feather, Leonard. **The Book of Jazz: A Guide to the Entire Field.** New York: Horizon Press, 1965.

————. **Inside Bebop.** New York: Robbins, 1949.

————. "Piano giants of jazz: Thelonius Monk," **Contemporary Keyboard,** 4 (1978): 55.

Gridley, Mark. **Jazz Styles.** Englewood Cliffs, NJ: Prentice-Hall, 1978.

Grove, Dick. **Basic Harmony and Theory as Applied to Improvisation.** Studio City, CA: Dick Grove Publications, 1971.

Hentoff, Nat. **Jazz Is.** New York: Random House, 1976.

Hobson, Wilder. **American Jazz Music.** New York: Da Capo, 1975.

Hodier, Andre. **Jazz: Its Evolution and Essence.** Translated by W. David Noakes. New York: Da Capo, 1975.

Kinkle, Roger. **The Complete Encyclopedia of Popular Music and Jazz, 1900-1950.** New Rocehlle, NY: Arlington House, 1974.

Koch, Lawrence. "Ornithology, a study of Charlie Parker's music, part 1," **Journal of Jazz Studies,** 2 (1974): 61–87.

―――. "Ornithology, a study of Charlie Parker's music, part 2," **Journal of Jazz Studies,** 2 (1975): 61–85.

Levey, Joseph. **Basic Jazz Improvisation.** Delaware Water Gap, PE: Shawnee Press, 1971.

Lindsay, Martin. **Teach Yourself Jazz.** London: English Universities Press, 1958.

Mehegan, John. **Contemporary Styles for the Jazz Pianist.** 3 vols. New York: Sam Fox, 1964–1970.

―――. **Jazz Improvisation.** 4 vols. New York: Watson-Guptill, 1959–1965.

―――. **The Jazz Pianist: Studies in the Art and Practice of Jazz Improvisation.** 3 vols. New York: Sam Fox, 1960–1966.

―――. **Styles for the Jazz Pianist.** 3 vols. New York: Sam Fox, 1961–1962.

Miedema, Harry. **Jazz Styles and Analysis: Alto Sax.** Chicago: Maher Publications, 1975.

Miles Davis Jazz Improvisation. Tokyo: Nichion, 1975.

Niehaus, Lennie. **Jazz Improvisation for Saxophone.** Hollywood: Try Publishing, 1972.

Ostransky, Leroy. **Understanding Jazz.** Englewood Cliffs, NJ: Prentice-Hall, 1977.

Pease, Frederick. **Jazz-Rock Theory.** Boston: Berklee Press, 1974.

Russell, George. **The Lydian Chromatic Concept of Tonal Organization for Improvisation.** New York: Concept, 1959.

Seargeant, Winthrop. **Jazz, Hot and Hydrid.** New York: Da Capo, 1975.

Schuller, Gunther. **Early Jazz: Its Roots and Musical Development.** New York: Oxford University Press, 1968.

Schwartz, S. **Jazz Improvisation.** Los Angeles: Charles Hansen II, 1975.

Shaw, Woody. "My approach to the trumpet and to jazz." **Crescendo International** 15 (1976/1977): 14–15.

Stanton, Kenneth. **Introduction to Jazz Theory: A Beginning Text in Harmony in Workbook Form.** Boston: Crescendo Publishing, 1976.

Tanner, Paul, and Gerow, Maurice. **A Study of Jazz.** 2d ed. Dubuque: Wm. C. Brown, 1973.

Tirro, Frank. **Jazz: A History.** New York: W. W. Norton, 1977.

Ulanov, Barry, **A History of Jazz in America.** New York: Viking Press, 1952.

Voight, John, and Kane, Randall. **Jazz Music in Print.** Winthrop, MA: Flat Nine Music, 1975.

White, Andrew. **The Works of John Coltrane.** 10 vols. Washington, D.C.: Andrew's Musical Enterprises, n.d.

Williams, Martin. **The Art of Jazz.** New York: Oxford University Press, 1959.

Wolking, Henry. "Jazz theory and functional harmony." **NAJE Educator** 11 (1979): 82–83.

index